BERNHARD LANGER

Centre for
Faith and Spirituality
Loughborough University

BERNHARD LANGER

My Autobiography

Written with Stuart Weir

Hodder & Stoughton
LONDON SYDNEY AUCKLAND

First published in Great Britain in 2002
This paperback edition first published in 2003

5

British Library Cataloguing in Publication Data
A record for this book is available from the British Library

ISBN 0 340 78716 3

Typeset in Baskerville BE Regular by Avon DataSet Ltd,
Bidford-on-Avon, Warwickshire

Printed and bound in Great Britain by
Clays Ltd, St Ives plc

Hodder & Stoughton
A Division of Hodder Headline Ltd
338 Euston Road
London NW1 3BH
www.madaboutbooks.com

Contents

1	Early life	1
2	Playing golf for a living	11
3	First successes	19
4	Challenging on the world stage	27
5	The US Masters 1985	40
6	The majors	52
7	The Ryder Cup	59
8	Putting problems	78
9	Success and despair in the late 1980s	85
10	The early 1990s	91
11	A memorable Easter Sunday	103
12	Developments in the game	107
13	Success with a long handle	114
14	Payne Stewart	125
15	Money – the 'root of all evil'?	128
16	Moving to the USA	137
17	What makes me tick?	141
18	Great golfers	153
19	The 2001 season and beyond	159
20	The Ryder Cup 2002	165
21	The future	176
	Appendix	179
	Glossary	193
	Index of names	197

Chapter 1

Early life

I was born in Anhausen, near Augsburg in Southern Germany, on 27 August 1957, the third child in the Langer household. How the Langer family came to set up home in Anhausen is something of a story in itself.

In September 1945 my father, Erwin, found himself herded with a group of other prisoners of war onto a train bound for Siberia. Somewhere along the journey, the train jolted to a stop. Erwin was cold, frightened and hungry. He did not know where the train had reached.

The French soldiers guarding the prisoners were less committed to their task than they should have been and this gave the prisoners their opportunity. When the train started to move again Erwin and several of the men decided to take charge of their own destiny. As the train struggled up a hill just short of the Czech border, they jumped from the carriage and ran into the darkness. As they raced for cover the soldiers on the train were shooting at them. Fortunately the bullets missed and the men made their escape.

It was one thing to be off the train. The next problem was how to survive without being re-captured. During the next few months my father scraped together a living by working on farms in the area.

My father's family had farmed an area of Sudetenland, a German-speaking region later to become part of Czechoslovakia, for a hundred years or so. My father would in all probability have spent his life on the family farm but for the outbreak of the Second World War. In 1938 he had been conscripted to the German army. In 1945 he was captured and held in a prisoner-of-war camp before being put on that train.

In April 1946 he wrote a letter to his parents, telling them what had happened to him and where he was. A few weeks later he got a reply, saying that things were hard with them and the Russians were taking over their farm with no compensation. They advised Erwin to stay in Germany. A few months later he heard from his parents that they had moved to a village called Anhausen. In September 1946 Erwin rejoined his parents.

Erwin Langer became a bricklayer and found work building houses in the area. The following year he met a local girl, Walburga or Wally. In 1949 they were married, and after a few years they started a family. Their first-born was also named Erwin. Then two years later my sister Maria came along and finally, three years later, I was born.

My childhood was a happy one. I had wonderful parents and a happy home, but it was not easy for my parents. Money was always in short supply. We did not have a family car. I never received any pocket money and had to wear my brother's hand-me-downs.

My father worked hard to support the family and my mother also did odd jobs to supplement the family income. I didn't lack any material things at the time and was just happy playing with friends and being out enjoying nature. Ironically it was the lack of money at home that set me on the road to a career in golf.

My father never made much of his wartime experience and only told the story when asked. He clearly had extraordinary strength of character and determination. I think I have inherited some of those characteristics, which stood me in good stead when the odds against me making it in golf seemed high.

I was very fortunate to grow up in a religious family. My

parents believed in God and I went to church every day, not just Sunday. I was an altar boy at seven years old and that really laid the foundation for my Christian belief later on. All my life I have believed in God.

I followed the rules and was very religious but I didn't realise my need for a personal relationship with God. By religious, I mean that I tried to keep all the rules, such as not eating meat on Fridays, going to church as often as possible and going to confession. All of these things are good but, according to the Bible, they will not get you into heaven.

My parents managed to finance the basics for the family but there were very few luxuries. As they could not afford to give us pocket money, we had to earn it. My brother and sister, Erwin and Maria, had discovered that there was money to be made at the local golf club, caddying for the members.

At the age of eight and a half, I followed Erwin to the Augsburg Golf Club, five miles away in the village of Burgwalden. I received lengthy and detailed instructions from my older brother on how to caddie – what to do, what not to do. Erwin had assured the club that I was well versed in the game of golf and the duties of a caddie. The procedure was then that you waited at the caddie shed until a member came along wanting a caddie. That day I experienced one of those lucky breaks that sometimes happen through just being in the right place at the right time.

The first person to ask for a caddie was Manfred Seidel who, I was to discover, was the club champion, with a handicap of three. He was very patient with me, as I am sure I did a lot wrong on that first day. Erwin's assurances that I had a thorough knowledge of golf could hardly have been further from the truth! Manfred was sufficiently satisfied with my performance to ask me to caddie for him again and so my association with the game of golf started. The 2.50 DM that he gave me at the end of the round probably meant more to me than any winner's cheque I have received since.

While Erwin saw caddying as just a way of making money, I was quite soon hooked on the game of golf. I watched the members closely and tried to learn everything I could about the game. School finished at noon and, as soon as I was free, I was off to the golf club, munching an apple and a sandwich as I cycled there. At weekends I would spend almost the whole day at the golf club.

In the summer holidays I would sometimes camp close to the course to avoid the five-mile cycle ride there and back. I became a popular caddie and gained a reputation for always being able to find my employer's ball, earning the nickname of 'Eagle Eyes'. As I got older I would sometimes double my income by carrying one player's bag while pulling a trolley for another, or pulling one trolley and pushing another.

There were eight boys from our town who caddied on a regular basis. Out of those eight, three became golf professionals.

I enjoyed having a little money to spend on myself, and saving the rest. At the same time, as I watched players on the course, my desire to try playing golf for myself was growing. As a caddie I was allowed to use the driving range, provided I did not inconvenience the members. The caddies had a collection of odd clubs, hand-me-downs from members. I spent hours on the practice ground, seeing what I could do myself.

The kids at school laughed at me when I told them I was going to be a golfer, because golf was not 'cool'. They had never heard of anybody going straight from school into professional golf and could not relate to me, a bricklayer's son, going into what was, at that time in Germany – and still is to a large extent – a rich man's game.

One of the club members gave us four old clubs, which all the caddies shared. There was a two wood, a three iron, a seven iron and a putter with a bent shaft. Maybe that's where all my putting problems came from!

As the clubs available did not include anything more lofted than a seven iron, I had to improvise. Learning to chip and pitch and play bunker shots with a seven iron may seem to have little relevance to playing tournament golf with a customised set of clubs. However, I am convinced that I have reaped great benefit throughout my career from the experience. Learning the art of shot-making and getting the ball close to the hole under difficult circumstances were useful skills that have stood me in good stead throughout my career.

There was a procedure for caddies to play on the course. You had to be able to play to a certain standard and be assessed by the professional. Three months after I had set foot on the golf course for the first time, and still a month short of my ninth birthday, I plucked up the courage to ask the pro, Sooky Maharaj – from Trinidad – to assess me. He told me to meet him at the practice ground early next morning. After I had hit about ten balls, he said I looked as if I could play on the course without doing it too much damage.

The first competition I ever played in was the annual caddies' championship. I did well without ever winning it, finishing in the top three several times. When I was fourteen I thought I had a great chance to win it and shot a 73, only to be beaten into second place by a shot.

That I was able to go round in 73 showed how I had progressed during my six years at the club. I had never had a lesson during that time and, in fact, my only learning aid was an eight-frame sequence of Jack Nicklaus's swing, a copy of which had been stuck up in the caddie shed. I tried to memorise this sequence and put it into practice on the range and the course. However, I am not sure that Jack would have recognised his swing in the scrawny teenager!

After four years of caddying, I had saved enough money for my first set of golf clubs, which were Kroydons – and boy, was I proud of them! They got polished and taken care of as if they were made of gold and diamonds.

I went to our local school where four grades were all in one room. After fifth grade, my parents decided to put me in a high school where I had to study all day so that I would have the same opportunity as my brother and sister. But I was so captivated by golf that I intentionally failed English and mathematics so I would be sent back to the school in our town. This meant I could continue going to the golf course every afternoon. Even then I had my priorities right!

At the age of fourteen, the end of my school life was in sight and I had to decide what I was going to do with my life. I was obsessed with golf and I wanted to be able to continue to play. However, as golf was at that time very much a game of the rich, if I found a normal job in Anhausen, there was no chance of my being able to afford membership of the club. It seemed that the only way I could remain in golf was if I could make golf my job.

In these days of dedicated golf channels and TV coverage of so many tournaments, it may be hard for the reader to understand how little I knew about the game in the late 1960s. There was no golf on television. Very occasionally I found a golf magazine, in English. I had heard of Jack Nicklaus and Arnold Palmer but scarcely anyone else.

When I told my parents I wanted to follow golf as my career, they thought I was mad and, not surprisingly, wanted me to have a proper job. My brother had gone to work as a tax advisor, my sister as a hotel receptionist. When I said I wanted to be a golf professional, my parents were against it. They thought I would make very little money and maybe, after two or three years, have no job at all. My father wanted me to get a decent job!

In my last summer as a caddie I earned enough to buy myself a new bike for 250 DM. That impressed my parents and perhaps encouraged them to let me consider golf as a career.

Another passion of my teenage years was football. I played for the Anhausen team and was a goal-scoring centre-forward.

I began supporting Bayern Munich, an allegiance I have retained ever since. As I grew older, golf and football were increasingly competing for my time. Football matches were on Saturday or Sunday, which were also the days on which I could earn most as a caddie. When I had to choose, more and more frequently I chose golf.

As I approached the time when I was to leave school, the idea of a job related to golf still really appealed to me. I went to the institute of job placement to see how they could help me with my career in golf. Eagerly, I stepped up to the placement officer's desk.

'What do you want to do?' he asked.

'I want to be a golf professional,' I replied.

'I've never heard of that,' he said as he walked into the next room to see if he could find any documents on such a profession.

I think I sat in the room for twenty minutes before he came back. He had a ruffled look on his face. 'There's no such thing as a golf professional,' he said. 'I would strongly advise you to find something else to do.'

One of the Augsburg golf club members used to go to Munich for lessons from a professional called Heinz Fehring at the Strasslach Club. One day the member told me that Heinz Fehring was looking for an assistant.

I telephoned Heinz Fehring. He seemed quite positive on the telephone and invited me to come to see him. I persuaded my parents to come with me to meet Heinz and the club president. The interview went well and they offered me the job. More importantly, they impressed my parents. The club found me a room with a family who lived close to the golf club and my mother also noticed that there was a Catholic church near by. In the end my parents agreed that I could take the job and pursue my dream.

The contract I signed was for three and a half years and my monthly salary was 350 DM a month in the first year, 400 DM the second and 450 DM in the last year. I had lessons from Heinz and played with him, watching him closely. I was, effectively, an apprentice professional and would start by learning my trade. I was still one month short of my fifteenth birthday so I was young to be leaving home – I was a boy embarking on a man's world. There were many times in the early days when I felt homesick. However, my dream was to be a golf professional and I was determined to give it a go.

That was August 1972. It was hard at first to leave home and live on my own in a rented room, but generally I had a great time, working in the golf club during the day and playing a lot of golf.

At first a major part of my duties was serving in the club shop. I had to go to the business school one day a week to study aspects of business. It was part of the final assessment of the golf professional to undertake an examination in English so I had to fit in English lessons as well.

However, to the credit of Heinz and his senior assistants, I was always given time to play a few holes or at least to hit some balls. After six months I was allowed to start giving lessons myself – maybe fifteen lessons each week – and some playing lessons on the course.

When I started as a professional at the age of fifteen, I had never had a lesson. Heinz Fehring immediately detected a number of faults. My grip was too strong. I needed to show fewer knuckles. I also had to work on my leg action as I was swinging round myself.

Heinz Fehring was like a second father to me. He helped me a lot with my golf game but he also helped me with my life. Away from home for the first time, I had no experience of life and little knowledge of how to conduct myself socially. He helped me to settle in and to develop as a person. It was also Heinz who introduced me to Willi Hoffman, who has been my coach for twenty-six years.

While I was at Munich I often played matches for money,

with the more wealthy, low-handicap members of the club. Before one such game, I hit some practice balls. The first swing shanked the ball. I put down a second ball, prepared to swing again and shanked that too. Incredibly, I shanked all fifty balls in the bucket. You can imagine the state I was in as I stepped on to the first tee! My first shot flew off the middle of my driver. I never looked back, went round in 69 and won the money. Why did I suddenly shank and why did it disappear so quickly again? I wish I knew.

Never having been an amateur, I did not have an official handicap. I would think that the standard of my play when I started as a professional was about one or two handicap. My game benefited, not only from Heinz's tuition, but also from the opportunity to play regularly on a good course, often in competition with the low-handicap members.

As I approached the end of my apprenticeship and my seventeenth birthday, Heinz asked me a very interesting question – in which way did I want to progress in my golf career? Did I want to become a club professional or a tournament pro? Of course, I knew it was a risk and I could not tell if I would be good enough, but I said that I wanted to be a tournament professional. I wanted to earn my living by my performance on the course. Heinz gave me every encouragement and altered my duties to give me more time to practise.

Shortly afterwards I was asked to play for Munich in an inter-club competition. It was a competition between four clubs, each represented by a team of amateurs and professionals. I was up against twenty-five of the best German professionals. I was only sixteen, but I managed to beat the other professionals to win the first prize of 500 DM. This was my first experience of tournament golf, and I was excited by the fact that in two days I had earned considerably more than in a month as an assistant club pro. It was a further indication that this was the route I should go.

I had my Golden Goose, centre-shafted putter stolen that year. It had been given to me by a member of the club, and was stolen by another member. I knew who had it but could not prove it, so I never got it back.

When I put my ball down on the first tee in the first round of my first German National, I was so nervous that I could hardly swing. I played a terrible shot, slicing the ball into the trees. My playing partner was a very experienced German amateur and he came over, put his arm around me and told me to relax and try to enjoy it. I chipped sideways on to the fairway and then took the eight iron and holed the ball! I am not sure who laughed more – me or my playing partner.

In 1975 the turning point came. In the German National Open at Cologne, I finished first equal with the World Cup international Gerhard Koenig and another bright youngster, twenty-year-old Manfred Kessler, and then won the play-off at the first sudden-death hole. I was the youngest-ever winner of that event.

Jan Brügelman, later to become president of the German Golf Federation, was watching that day. Heinz had told him that I was keen to try the European tour. Jan spoke to me about it, seemed interested and asked me to contact him again if I was going to play the tour.

I called him and he asked me to go and see him. I did so and he offered me a deal. He would pay me a monthly sum of money and I would give him 50 per cent of my prize money. I was very grateful and very excited.

When I finished with my apprenticeship and received my diploma as a head professional, I decided to try my luck on the European tour. Until then, no German had ever had any kind of success on the tour, and I really did not know what to expect and what kind of competition I would be facing.

Chapter 2

Playing golf for a living

When I play a tournament now, I fly to the venue, am picked up in a courtesy car and stay in a nice hotel. In 1976 it was a bit different.

Winning the 1975 German National Open earned me 6,000 DM with which I bought my first car, a bright yellow Ford Escort. My father could see now that golf was not such a bad job after all. In my car I set off to drive to Portugal for my debut on the European tour. I drove the 1,600 miles to Marbella in Spain, accomplishing the drive pretty much non-stop in twenty-five hours. After a few days' practice in Marbella, I drove on to Portugal to compete in the Portuguese Open.

There were two big differences in the tour then, compared to now. One was that, at that time, there were two cuts – after the second and third rounds. Also it was not an all-exempt tour. The top sixty in the previous year's money list were exempt; the rest had to qualify on a week-to-week basis. If you did not make the final day of the tournament (surviving both cuts) you had to pre-qualify for the next week's tournament, on the Monday. In those days the season was much shorter than it is now and there were only about twenty to twenty-five tournaments in the year.

When I joined the European tour in 1976 I had no idea what would happen and no clue what to expect. There were no German tour pros and no German had ever done well on the tour, so I had no one to measure myself against. I was hoping I would be good enough to make it but I had no way of knowing until I tried.

My first ambition was to make enough money to survive financially. In the longer term, of course, I hoped to win tournaments and become one of the top players. However, in the early days I had enough money to play only a few tournaments, so the first target was to make enough to be able to continue on the tour.

I had in fact played four tournaments on the European tour prior to 1976. In July 1974 I played in the Swiss Open in Crans-sur-Sierre. I shot 77 and 79 and missed the cut by six. The following month I played in the German Open at Krefeld and again missed the cut.

In 1975 I played in the German Open at Bremen. With rounds of 75 and 78, I survived the first cut but with a third-round 78 missed the third day cut by three shots. I also played in the Italian Open at Monticello in October and missed the cut.

The year 1976 was different in that I was planning to play a series of tournaments, one after another. At my first tournament in Portugal, I opened with a 73 and followed it with a 77. Unfortunately the scores were going in the wrong direction as the third round was a 79. I made the Friday cut, but not the Saturday one. So it was off to the Spanish Open at La Manga. Same story – made the first cut but missed the second one and no money. My scores of 76, 73 and 76 were two outside the cut.

The next tournament was the Madrid Open at Puerta de Hierro. The course requires long and straight hitting off the tee and accurate approach play. I not only made the cut but also finished fifth with 69, 76, 71 and 70 – eleven shots behind the winner, Francisco Abreu. You can imagine how thrilled I was!

I had set out three weeks earlier, not knowing how good I

was or what the required standard was. Here in my third tournament I had found that I was good enough to compete at that level. Unfortunately, before I had the chance to build on this success, serious putting problems began to develop – but that is another story. It tended to continue like that – missed cuts followed by good finishes and then another missed cut.

I made the first but not the second cuts at the French Open and the Swiss but missed the first cut at the Dutch. I was in the money at the German Open, finishing thirty-second with scores of 73, 71, 73 and 68.

The first two or three years on the European tour were pretty rough. I stayed in some terrible places – the cheapest I could find. I didn't want to spend much money on food, couldn't afford a caddie, and certainly could not afford to fly from country to country, so I spent many long hours on the road.

Jan Brügelman was paying me 1,700 DM a month in return for 50 per cent of all winnings. I was very grateful but it was not enough. To play in four tournaments in a month was costing about 2,500 DM. By the end of the year I was covering my costs. In addition to my £2,130 official prize money, I had made money in Germany. I was runner-up in defence of my national title in Nuremburg, but as the winner was an amateur, I collected the top prize of 6,000 DM. I added 5,000 DM by winning a Ratingen pro-am and won some smaller sums by winning other pro-ams.

I was the best German golfer, which was something, but that did not count for a great deal internationally.

My grip was very strong in those days, both hands to the right, which usually closes the club face. While I was certainly unorthodox, I can think of other players – for example, Paul Azinger, Fred Couples, David Duval or Lee Trevino – who have had a lot of success with a pretty strong grip. Often people have preconceptions about how you should play, but look at someone like Isao Aoki. The way he holds the putter and the way he swings, he should have no chance, but he has had a great career.

Even at that early stage I could see that my ball-striking was better than that of most of the guys. In this I was probably in the top 10 to 20 per cent, but in the short game and putting I was way down. I knew that my ball-striking was so good that if I could raise the standard of my short game I could be one of the best players. That was the encouragement I needed.

Alex Hay, the BBC commentator and former director of golf at Woburn, encountered me for the first time and made a comment about this point. Apparently, after watching me hit one or two shots, he wrote in his notebook, 'With a grip like that he will not go far in the game.' Before I had completed the round he had erased the note!

I think my good ball-striking was the result of good technique and proper compensation. It was also the result of a lot of hard work. I have been fortunate in that throughout my career I have always enjoyed practising. I was physically strong and I worked hard to hit the ball long and to control the shots.

As I competed week in, week out with seasoned pros I was able to assess myself – see how I measured up and where my weaknesses were. There were enough encouragements for me to believe I was not wasting my time pursuing the dream.

If my first target was to earn enough to survive on the tour, my second was to get exempt status, to avoid having to go through the qualifying process every week.

I had won tournaments in Germany and made a number of cuts, which provided enough money to keep me going. I finished ninetieth in the Order of Merit in 1976 – no great success but I had fulfilled the first target of financial survival and was on my way.

Gary Player was always my hero. I liked his approach to golf. He was a fitness fanatic and obsessive about practice –

just as I am. Once when Gary holed a bunker shot someone said, 'That was lucky!'

He replied, 'Yes, I am a lucky golfer. And you know, the more I practise, the luckier I become!'

He is about my size, which made it easier for me to relate to him and learn from his swing. I looked up to Gary a lot, probably more than to anybody else. Like me, he had a flattish swing. I could not copy that steep, upright, Nicklaus swing I'd seen in the caddie shed. That was no good to me.

In 1976 I had just pre-qualified for the Open Championship at Royal Birkdale for the first time. I was in the locker room when Gary asked me if I would like to join him for a practice round. Would I like to! He could not have been kinder to me that day, giving me advice on how to approach a major championship and how to play Birkdale. It was a great experience.

As we spent some time together, what struck me was that he was constantly trying something new and, as a result, he hit the ball all over the place. His golf was terrible. He looked as if he did not know what he was doing but, in the end, he played all four rounds. That impressed me.

Also in 1976 I was invited to play for Europe against Great Britain in the Hennessey Cup at Lille. This was my first experience of the matchplay format, which amateurs play in a great deal, but of course I had never been an amateur, going straight from being a caddie to being a pro. Sadly, my putting was so bad that I only played once. Unlike the Ryder Cup, not all players play the singles and I was omitted. My one outing was a four-ball and we lost five and four as Great Britain and Ireland ran away with the match 20–10.

In 1977 the aim would have been to build on the achievements of 1976. In reality 1977 largely passed me by as I was called up for the German air force. My national service began on 1 January and it put my golf career on hold. Having to serve in the air force was not at all what I wanted to do, but of course I had no choice.

Bad became worse when I went on a training exercise, which involved a ten-mile march in freezing cold conditions carrying a heavy backpack. Eventually we stopped for something to eat. Halfway through the meal we were told that an enemy plane was flying overhead – we had to throw ourselves on the ground. We must have done it fifty times. As I did so my backpack jarred my back severely. I had no choice but to continue the march. It was painful that evening but by the next morning I was unable to get out of bed. I was in hospital for two and a half weeks and thought my career had ended before it had really got started.

Fortunately, shortly after this I was posted to a unit of sportsmen and the duties were less demanding. I was allowed to spend some of my time practising my golf. Throughout my career I have had intermittent problems with my back, perhaps as a result of that incident on the military exercise.

I played in five European tour events in 1977 and was in the money in two of them, but that left me in a lowly 204th place in the official money list. I started with a 68 in the Swiss Open but fell away a bit to finish thirty-ninth. I missed the cut in the German Open but was twentieth in the Tournament Players' Championship (TPC) at Foxhills. In the Dutch Open, I made the cut and finished fifty-first – the bad news was that prize money stopped at fiftieth!

Defending the German National Open, I averaged forty putts per round. At the second hole in the first round, I hit my approach to six feet, then took four putts. I hit my first putt so hard that I double-hit it. It finished less than a foot from the hole but I missed that one too.

I played a full season again in 1978, with sixteen tournaments and finished fortieth on the money list with £7,006. It was a season in which I improved as it progressed. I started with missed cuts at the Portuguese and Spanish but was forty-sixth at the Madrid Open. Then I was out of the money in the French and Martini but was twenty-third in the

Belgian Open and then missed three more cuts including the German Open.

After that bleak start to the season – I had played nine tournaments and only made two cuts – things could only improve. In the remaining six tournaments I not only made five cuts but collected £1,000 cheques in four of them. I was seventh in the Benson and Hedges International Open at Fulford, four shots behind Lee Trevino; seventh in the Tournament Players' Championship, six behind Brian Waites; and eighth in the Irish Open at Portmarnock, four behind Ken Brown.

I was twentieth in the European Open at Walton Heath. This was a tournament with big prize money. The winner, Bobby Wadkins, took home £18,000 – Jack Nicklaus only made £12,500 for winning the Open Championship that year. The good news for me was that twentieth still qualified me for over £1,000!

I played in the Open Championship at St Andrews that year. With scores of 78 and 73, I missed the cut by three. I was one behind Johnny Miller. When I played in the Open Championship in 1976 Johnny Miller won it. It was a timely reminder that golf is no respecter of persons or reputations.

I played in the Cacharel Under-25s Championship and came eleventh. I also represented West Germany in the World Cup in Hawaii, where the US team of John Mahaffey and Andy North won.

In 1978, I was again selected for the Hennessey Cup at the Belfry. It was altogether more enjoyable as I was much more involved than in 1976 and the final result was much closer, with Great Britain and Ireland only winning 17½ to 14½.

Manúel Piñero and I beat Mark James and Howard Clark in the four-ball but lost to Nick Faldo and John O'Leary in the foursome. I won a tough single with Bernard Gallacher on the eighteenth green.

The twelve players who were in each team for the Hennessey Cup were given an exemption on the tour for two years. So that was my second target achieved. I had exempt status in 1979 and 1980.

Chapter 3

First successes

For me, 1979 was an up-and-down year. I made cuts more consistently than ever but without being in contention. Of fourteen tournaments played, I made twelve cuts but was typically finishing thirtieth to fortieth. I dropped to fifty-sixth in the money list but actually made more money than I had in the previous year.

My best performance on the tour was fifth place in the Swiss Open. I also took second place in the individual event in the World Cup in Greece behind Hale Irwin as the USA retained their title. However, the season was transformed by four days in France.

I won the Cacharel World Under-25s Tournament at Nîmes by seventeen strokes. This was a record for a professional tournament, beating by sixteen strokes the previous record of Bobby Locke in the 1948 Chicago Victory National tournament. My scores were 73, 67, 67, 67. Among those I beat was Nick Faldo. Having gone into the tournament low in confidence in my putting, that week I just made every putt I looked at.

It was not a regular European tour event but it was significant because it was a worldwide field in my age group, and also because I won it by such a large margin. It showed me that I could beat anyone my age in the world – if I could get my game together. It wasn't as if I just sneaked through on the wire – I won it by some margin. This was another step on the ladder of finding out how good I was and how far I could go. I knew I could win in Germany but this was my first success on the international stage.

I approached 1980 with added confidence. In the winter I played the South American tour of five tournaments. I did not win any of them but was in the top five in each, and topped the money list.

However, the 1980 European season started very much like the previous one. In the first fifteen tournaments I made thirteen cuts but had only one top-ten finish; I was missing so many short putts. I came fifth in the European Open but that was my only top-ten finish until then.

In September I was playing in the Hennessey Cup at Sunningdale. Again Europe lost 13½ to 16½. I had a good week. Playing with Antonio Garrido, we won two foursomes. I also played three singles, one each day. I beat Eddie Polland 4 and 3 and Sam Torrance 5 and 4, but lost to Mark James on the eighteenth despite four birdies (one shot less than the score expected on the hole).

Something very significant happened that week. I was on the putting green when Seve (Severiano Ballesteros) took my putter, tried it and gave it back, saying, 'Horrible putter.'

I said, 'What do you mean – "Horrible putter"? I have been using this putter all year.'

He said, 'Too light and not enough loft.'

Now at that stage, Seve was the best player in Europe so I took seriously what he said.

I went into the pro shop and said that I was looking for a new putter. I looked at all the putters in the shop, including the second-hand ones. I picked up an old one and said, 'How much is this?' The pro said it was £5. He said it had belonged to an old lady who just wanted to get rid of it. It was an Acushner Bull's Eye, a woman's centre-shafted putter. I borrowed it, tried a few putts and bought it. Using that old putter in the next three tournaments I improved dramatically. So it was £5 well spent. Thanks, Seve!

The next three tournaments turned my year round. The first tournament I played with the new putter was the Haig Whisky Tournament Players' Championship. I was second, three shots behind Bernard Gallacher. It was an odd tournament for me with scores of 71, 64, 71 and 65.

The following week I was fifth in the Bob Hope British Classic. I could feel that I was getting closer and closer to winning – if you finish second, you are not far away. The first time you are in contention you usually mess up because you are not used to the pressure. I was getting closer and learning. That was certainly true that week. With 66, 67 and 67 I was second, but with a final round 71 I lost ground.

The next tournament – and also the last of the year – was the Dunlop Masters at St Pierre, Chepstow, in Wales. The pre-tournament favourites were Sandy Lyle and Greg Norman, who were battling for top spot on the European tour money list. An American, Hubert Green, put all that in the shadows with an opening 67. A second round 77 left Hubert struggling. I followed my opening 70 with a 65 to take the lead. That was quite a round – eleven fours and seven threes. I went forty-one successive holes without dropping a shot in this tournament.

A third round of 67 maintained my lead. On the final day I was paired with Brian Barnes, who was one of the established players on the tour. I remember thinking, 'I want to win so badly.' I was in contention and I was very nervous. I realised that winning a European tour event would move me up a level and open all sorts of doors for me.

When it happened, I was extremely relieved as much as happy. I played well on the Sunday, hitting most of the fairways and shot a good 68. The 'new' putter did a good job as I averaged only 27 putts a round that week.

I finished ninth in the European money list. At the end of the season I again went back to South America and won the

Colombian Open. It wasn't the most significant tournament in the world, but it was another stepping-stone on the road.

I was invited to play a tournament in Brazil. However, as the first prize was only $8,000, I could have finished well up the tournament and not have covered my expenses. The organisers were keen to have me so they threw in a return airfare and hotel. That was, I suppose, my first experience of appearance money.

The following year, 1981, saw me break through to another level. I took a number of steps forward. I topped the European money list, came second in the Open Championship and won my first German Open. No one would have ever thought a German could do that. Oh, yes, we have good football players, great tennis stars, good skiers, but golf? No way!

I played seventeen official European tournaments and won twice, with eleven top-five finishes and fourteen out of seventeen in the top ten. It was a great year, but I was also a little disappointed to have been second six times, as some of those had been there for the winning. It is an indication of how far the tour has moved on that I topped the money list and won £81,000. Ten years later, you could get £80,000 for finishing second or third in one tournament.

Winning the German Open was very important for me, as no German had ever won it in the seventy years of its history and to win in my home country was very pleasing. It also put a lot of extra pressure on me, I remember – having so many friends and relatives all wanting me to win. So you have the pressure not just of the tournament, but also not letting your friends down. What is important for me is to do my job and not to allow seeing all my friends to distract me. With rounds of 67, 69 and 64, I took a decent lead into the final round and just held on with a 72 for a one-shot win over Tony Jacklin, whose final round was 67.

I cannot really explain why I have had so many successes in Germany. People say to me, 'You are obviously trying really hard.' That is true, but I try really hard in every tournament. I do not know whether it has anything to do with the fact that more people walk with me and are wanting me to win than in other countries. But that doesn't explain it either, as I have lots of followers in England and in other countries. I am comfortable with everything in Germany, but I have also lived a lot in the USA and I like it there too.

I am fortunate in feeling comfortable in most countries. I enjoy a variety of food and never have difficulty eating as I travel. I don't like the showers in England but that doesn't stop me playing well there! In Germany or the USA you turn on the shower and you are wet in two seconds; in England it is more like two minutes.

One thing that is different about playing in Germany is that I always have to go to the press conference. Normally the press only want to talk to the tournament leader and anyone who's done something special, but they always want me whether I've shot 60 or 80. Sometimes that bugs me when I have had a bad day. I'm thinking, 'I have just shot 80. Why do you want to talk to me?'

There are a lot of demands on my time when I'm playing in Germany. I don't just have to do one press conference – every TV station and radio station in the country wants to talk to me. Sometimes I go from one to the next, to the next and so on. Then I may have to fit in a photo shoot, make an appearance for a sponsor and go to a dinner party. Without a doubt, German tournaments are the most demanding ones for me. When I play in another country, I play my golf, do the press conference and then I'm free. In Germany I am busy from morning to night.

Maybe that's the secret! When I'm busy from morning to night and exhausted, perhaps that is what makes me play well.

I won the Bob Hope British Classic at Moor Park with rounds of 67, 65, 68, beating Peter Oosterhuis by one. The tournament was reduced to fifty-four holes by the weather. I was second in the Open Championship at Sandwich. My scores were 73, 67, 70 and 70. I was two behind at halfway, but five behind after three rounds and lost by four. I was never quite going to win it, but it was another landmark.

I had played in the Open Championship three times but had never done well. It was the only major I had ever played. Being in contention in the Open just showed me that I could compete with the best in the world on a tough golf course. It gave me the confidence to believe that I could win it one day. The £17,500 for coming second was my biggest cheque so far.

In 1981 I became a world-famous golfer in a rather amusing way. I was playing in the Benson and Hedges International at Fulford. On the seventeenth hole I hit a nine iron to the green, pulled it left and it hit a big oak tree, to the left of the green. I heard the ball hit two or three times but did not see it come down. Seconds later the spectators started laughing and, sure enough, the ball was lodged in a little indentation in a branch about fifteen feet up!

I was in contention – finishing second in the end. My only concern was how to play the hole best – to make a par (average score for the hole, including two putts) or at worst bogey (one above par for the hole), and not double (two above par for the hole) or worse. As I walked to the green I was thinking, 'What are my options?' The options were to go back and replay the shot, with a penalty; to take a drop under the tree, again with a penalty shot; or to play as it lay.

The worst option was to go back and take a 'stroke and distance' penalty. Dropping a ball at the green side was a better option, but still with a penalty. The best option, if it were possible, was clearly to play the ball from where it lay. I considered the options, looked where the ball was and decided that I might be able to hit it onto the green.

The hardest part was getting up the tree, getting a stance, and especially not falling out of the tree as I hit the ball! I managed to succeed in hitting the ball onto the green, leaving myself a putt for par. The crowd went absolutely crazy. Unfortunately I missed it, but at least it was only one dropped shot.

My only concern was to get the best score on the hole, and it was a bonus that there was a TV camera behind the hole – remember, in those days they only covered the last few holes. It was shown on TV around the world and, as I was pretty much at the beginning of my career, I was in some places better known for climbing the tree than for my golf!

In fact my ball has stuck up a tree three times in my career. The second and third times were both in California, most recently at the end of 2001, and both Peter Coleman (my caddie) and I were in the tree, though Peter went higher. As I definitely could not play the ball this time, there was no point in my climbing up. It was a three wood that struck the ball high up in the tree, where it stuck maybe sixty feet up. You could see the ball from underneath but you could not get to it.

The next problem in this situation is that, under the rules, I have to be able to identify my ball. I could see it was a Titleist but every tournament player marks his ball in a particular way. I put two dots by the number. The referee said, 'If you are not sure that is your ball, you have to go back and replay the shot.'

I said, 'I know it is my ball. I saw it go there and get stuck.'

He said, 'Can you identify it?'

I said, 'No, but I know it is my ball.'

So we got binoculars from someone in the crowd and with them we could see the two dots on the ball, and so I was allowed to drop it under the tree. After I declared it unplayable, we shook the tree and the ball fell.

I had my first experience of playing in the USA in 1981 when I was invited to play in the World Series. I was leading with six holes to play but could not quite sustain it. It was a good experience and again boosted my confidence. That was shortly after the Benson and Hedges tournament and the tree incident.

I was amused to overhear this conversation between two people in the gallery:

'Who is that?'

'Isn't he the man who climbs trees?'

'What's his name?'

'I think it's Bernard-something.'

'No, it's not. That's Tarzan!'

I also made my Ryder Cup debut in 1981, which was a great experience.

Chapter 4

Challenging on the world stage

In 1981 I was officially the best golfer in Europe. That was another of my goals met. The question now was, could I sustain it and even move on to a higher level? At that time I was completely focused on golf. I had no kids. I was unmarried. There was just me and my job.

Don't misunderstand me – I love my wife and kids more than I can express, but the simple fact is, there are now so many distractions. I hope I have got the balance right in terms of giving to my family without detriment to my fitness or my golf. But it is a balancing act and often one aspect suffers – my family or my golf, my fitness or my time with God. There are only so many hours in the day and you have to fit it all in.

I also know now, if I did not know it then, that playing well in one tournament is no guarantee that you will play well in the next. You can take nothing for granted in golf. Often last week's tournament winner will miss the cut this week and even finish twenty shots worse.

Part of the reason is that we play on different golf courses, in different countries, in different climates, sometimes fighting jet-lag. One week we play in calm conditions, the next week it is a links course with strong winds. There can be different sand in the bunkers, different grass on the greens. All this makes it hard for one player to win two or three tournaments in a row.

* * *

For me, 1982 was an up-and-down year. I had a win and two second places, and finished sixth in the money list. Having become the first German ever to win my national Open, I successfully defended it at the Solitude Club near Stuttgart, but it was not easy. After opening rounds of 73 and 71, I found myself seven behind leader Christy O'Connor Jnr.

It was a very hard week for me because the crowds were running about everywhere and photographers took pictures whenever they wanted, several times during the backswing or before impact. Golf in Germany was new and the photographers needed good pictures. However, they had no experience of how to work at a golf tournament. Because of all this nobody wanted to play with me.

A 69 in the third round narrowed the gap but I was still three off the lead. In the final round I mounted a real Arnold Palmer charge with six threes in eleven holes (five birdies and eight single-putts in a round of 66). I won the play-off with Bill Longmuir at the first extra hole.

It was nice to win the play-off, having lost a play-off to Tony Jacklin in the Sun Alliance Professional Golfers' Association (PGA) Championship at Hillside when Tony all but holed his second shot at the first extra hole. That was probably the most depressing moment in my career so far because I played so well and putted so badly.

Time and time again, I rifled second shots within six feet of the flag and time after time I comprehensively missed the cup. I was still leading with three to play, but took four putts from the edge of the green for a five at the par-three sixteenth to allow Jacklin to level matters.

I had a solid performance in the Open Championship, finishing thirteenth and six shots behind Tom Watson.

It was about this time that I began my partnership with Peter Coleman, who has caddied for me now for over twenty years. Peter approached me in 1981. His professional attitude impressed me from the first day. He is always on time, always immaculately turned out and totally committed. No matter how long I want to practise, he never complains.

Peter's route into golf was not unlike mine. He started off caddying to earn pocket money. On leaving school he worked in an office but left that quickly when he had a chance to work as an assistant at a golf club. After a further spell in a 'proper' job, he got a chance to caddie for Tommy Horton and took it. He also worked for Nancy Lopez and Seve. After a brief association in 1982 he went to work for Greg Norman, but returned to me in 1983 and we have been together ever since.

It is not easy to get along with someone for that length of time. There is a lot of pressure. There can be conflict in the heat of the moment. I accuse him of things from time to time. That is part of caddying. Sometimes I need to let off steam and he just has to take it to protect me. A good caddie needs a thick skin sometimes. It is in the caddie's long-term interest to take it from the player if that helps the player to do well, because a caddie earns more from a winning player.

Everything is quite different today from when I started. Now you can buy yardage books that have been done professionally and that you can rely on. But when Peter and I started working together, these were not available.

We often do the yardages together. These days we normally need to do no more than to check the published yardage books. We use a laser to measure. If there is a hole where we are not happy with the published distances, I will go to the green and Peter hits me with a laser and we know the distance. Most of the time the books are so accurate that we don't need to change anything. The way we operate most of the time is that both of us have the same book.

It is easy to make mistakes under the pressure of a tournament. For example, the book tells you it is 160 yards from a sprinkler; you walk forward twelve yards, but you add when you should be subtracting and get 172 instead of 148. You then take the wrong club and go right through the green. With both player and caddie checking the distance, that is less likely to happen.

Choice of club is crucial. As well as the distance there are factors such as the wind, the lie, whether the shot is uphill or downhill, to consider. It also depends on how I want to hit the shot. I need to consider if I want to hit it straight or with draw or fade, as that can make the difference of one club. Peter and I talk about it. Most of the time we agree and most of the time it is an easy decision.

There are times when Peter may say six iron and I don't feel right about that – I want to hit a five. In the end I'm the one who has to hit the shot, so I must be comfortable with it. Perhaps, too, Peter does not want to be blamed!

In 1983 I had three wins, a second and a third, to finish third in the order of merit. The first win was in the Italian Open at Ugolino, where four sub-70 rounds left me in a tie with Ken Brown and Seve. I won the play-off at the second extra hole.

It is pretty nerve-racking to be in a play-off, but I would rather that than not. You have to accept that play-offs are not always fair. They are played under intense pressure. It is one good shot and you win, one bad shot and you lose. It is fascinating. It's what you work for, practise for – to get into those situations where you can win tournaments.

In play-offs you have somehow to be aggressive and, at the same time, to play safe. You have to go for it, as there is no second chance; you are thinking that par is probably not going to be good enough as someone will probably make birdie. Equally, you don't want to be too aggressive and make bogey when par might be good enough.

It is match play, so you are looking at where the others are lying. If the others are in trouble, there is no need to try to pull off the miracle shot and get yourself into trouble.

Over the years I have been in a lot of play-offs. In 1992 in the BMW tournament, I was in a five-player play-off. It was a very unusual experience for five players to drive off together. The first hole we played was a short par-four. I felt that someone was going to make birdie. Ironically it was Paul Azinger who played the worst tee shot. He was in the rough with a downhill lie while the rest of us had pitching wedges from the fairway – but he made birdie and we didn't.

The 1986 Trophée Lancôme was another strange play-off. I tied with Seve, over seventy-two holes. After four holes of the play-off we were still tied and it was getting dark. We had played seventeen, eighteen and then seventeen, eighteen again and we were both two or three under but still level. The officials and players discussed the situation. Both Seve and I had commitments the next day so we agreed to share first prize. That was such an unusual thing to happen. History was to repeat itself in 2002 but this is another story.

In 1983 I also won the Glasgow Golf Classic, beating Vicente Fernandez by a shot and the St Mellion Timeshare Tournament Players' Championship, where I secured victory with two closing 66s. I was runner-up in the Benson and Hedges International, beaten only with an eagle (two under par for the hole) putt by John Bland on the eighteenth. The year also included a good Ryder Cup performance.

I started to travel. I played a few tournaments in the USA and then won in Japan, the Casio World Open. This was good, for it gave me a bit more experience of playing in different conditions. I suppose it also gave me some more exposure around the world. All of this helped me to believe in myself, that I could be successful wherever I played.

As an established player, looking back, a lot of these achievements don't seem very significant, but you need to remember that, at this stage, I was just learning my trade. Each small step took me to the next level and showed me that I could move on to the next one.

The tournament with the longest lasting effect that year was one I played but missed the cut in Florida. At the end of one day's play, I bumped into a very attractive girl from Louisiana called Vikki. After a brief conversation I asked her out to dinner. Not surprisingly, as we had just met, she said no.

However, a little later she ended up inviting me to join a group of eight people she was going out with that night. I was due to leave for Germany the next week but, having met Vikki, I ended up staying another week, and then we dated long-distance.

Vikki came to Europe for three weeks – her first visit – and I showed her around. It was a wonderful time. Only six months after meeting me she agreed to give up her job and to travel with me. In September 1983 we got engaged and were married on 20 January 1984. That was the beginning of many great things.

As Vikki's parents were no longer alive, we were married in Anhausen, in the church where I had served as an altar boy. It was a small wedding but attracted quite a lot of media attention – there seemed to be almost as many photographers as there were guests! There were also some surprises for Vikki in the way we do weddings in Germany.

Vikki's first surprise was the wedding cake. She was expecting a layered cake with white icing, but our cake was in dark chocolate. The second surprise was when she was 'kidnapped'. The tradition is that the bride is kidnapped and the groom has to find her. Fortunately, Anhausen is not big and I found her quite quickly. She was with my brother and some other friends at the local tennis club, drinking champagne – which the tradition required me to pay for!

After we were married, it was life on the tour – home for less than half the year. It was an odd life, but the only one we knew.

They were good years. The golf was good, we were young and it was fun. That Vikki loved to travel was a big help.

When our daughter, Jackie, was born two years later, life changed completely. It was different on the road with a baby, and with two, and then three kids, the travelling became even more difficult. When Jackie and then the others reached school age, we faced different problems.

For eight years we home-schooled Jackie at the beginning and end of the school year. Then later we also home-schooled Stefan and Christina for two full years. You just do what you have to do to make things work. I think that is the key to this lifestyle. Whatever works for you is the answer, and you just get on with it.

When we first got married, our intention was to live in Germany, but the first year we were married I played eight events on the US tour, won $80,000, and received my US tour card for 1985. So we bought a house in Boca Raton, Florida, and spent six months in Europe and six in the USA. That was nice – we had the best of both cultures and avoided cold winters. Then as the years went on, we spent less and less time in Europe and more in America.

1984 was another successful year. I won four national Opens – French, Dutch, Spanish and Irish. Again I finished top of the European Order of merit and I was second in the Open Championship at St Andrews.

My victory in the French Open was not an easy one. I started 68 and 71 but was hitting the ball badly and spraying shots all over the place. Someone offered to film me with his video camera. From the video I could see I was coming over the ball. I phoned my coach, Willi Hoffmann, in Stuttgart and checked with him what I should do to cure it. We had four long conversations and, by the third round, I'd solved it. I shot 67.

I was also missing too many putts. I thought my alignment

was all right but in fact I was way out. I practised for two hours on the Saturday evening and decided to try a new method of placing the blade behind the ball and standing square to the hole to check I was lined up properly, then walking round to the putting position. I was a little worried that it might be against the rules, but I got the OK from tournament director Tony Gray. With a final round sixty-four I beat José Rivero by one and Nick Faldo by three.

I won the Dutch Open at Arnhem by four shots from Graham Marsh, effectively winning with my first round of 64. The round contained only 22 putts, though it should have been a 62 as it contained a double bogey on a par-five and might easily have been a 61.

I was second in the PGA Championship at Wentworth. My scores were all in the 60s but winner Howard Clark didn't give the rest of us much chance with his opening 64. The tournament was shortened to fifty-four holes by the weather.

I won the Irish Open with rounds of 68, 66, 67 and 66, beating Mark James by four. Afterwards Mark paid tribute to my short game. He said I had the best short game in Europe and that I could get up and down from a lady's handbag. Thanks, Mark, I appreciate the compliment but I have to confess that I have never tried the handbag shot!

The Spanish Open of 1984 at El Saler, a superb links course carved out of the rugged coastline near Valencia, is a tournament that is forever etched on my mind. I was robbed, and fined for slow play, I shot my lowest round ever and won the tournament! I opened with rounds of 73 and 68. A thief entered our room while Vikki was having a tennis lesson and took most of our personal belongings. Vikki did not tell me until after my round, which was a 72. I was so angry I hardly slept that night.

As far as the slow play fine was concerned, the round took four hours and forty minutes and we finished ten minutes behind schedule. It was the first and only time I've been disciplined for slow play in over twenty-five years on the European tour. I know I'm not the fastest player in the game, but I'm not the slowest either. I was playing with Seve – in Spain – and that is not easy. You have to push your way through the crowds. If they were watching my time, why didn't any officials warn me?

While we are on the subject of slow play, I recognise that I am on the slow side. I feel that I am meticulous – like Nicklaus. People are made differently; some of us just need a little more time before we are ready to pull the trigger. And I am one who likes to take a little more time. Equally, I would want to say that I have played for ten to fifteen years in an environment where there are strict rules on timing – forty seconds for a shot. But I have only been fined once in Europe and once in America, very early in my career – and that was because I was facing a very difficult shot. I was in the trees, looking for a narrow gap and having to carry water. I have not been fined since.

It is not that I like to stand around. In fact, I like to play at a steady pace. I do take my time over shots, to take account of every factor I can – distance, lie, wind, pin position and so on. One bad shot, perhaps caused by not taking everything into account, can cost you two or three strokes, which may be the difference between first and tenth place.

When I need to speed up, I walk faster. When it is my turn to go I am usually ready. But if I play at my own pace, I recognise that I am a little slower than most players. That is just my routine and how I like to play, but of course I have to play within the rules, and I try to do that.

It might surprise you, but I prefer to play with fast players than with slow ones. If I am drawn to play with two slow players, then we are in trouble! If you put three of the slower players in one group then it's inevitable that they are going to struggle not to fall behind. So it is better for me to be with faster players so that I never fall behind.

Getting back to the Spanish Open, the fine, the robbery and everything meant that I was not best pleased when I set out on my final round, seven shots behind Howard Clark. I shot a 62 with only 24 putts, to win the tournament, beating Howard by one.

I didn't honestly think 62 was possible – it was my best-ever round at that stage of my career. I'd had a ten-under round once before, in a pro-am at Moor Park, but never on so tough a course or when the pressure was on. So 1984 was my year of low scores as I also shot a 66 in Italy (six under); and a 65 in Switzerland (seven under); as well as the 64 in Holland and the 62 in Spain.

I told the press afterwards that I had to win the tournament as that was the only way I could break even on the week. My caddie, Peter, was delighted too as it meant that I would be able to pay him!

One other quaint aspect of that week was that I captained a Rest of the World XI football team in a 2–2 draw against a Spanish side led by Seve. I was described in *Golf Weekly* as 'a lively left-winger'. Thanks – but I decided not to give up the day job.

I had a good run at the Suntory World Matchplay championship at Wentworth. I like playing Wentworth. A feature of the course is that there is a lot of undulation. There are a number of long, demanding holes, such as the first, third, thirteenth and fifteenth, but then there are also some short par-fours such as the sixth, seventh, eighth, sixteenth and, of course, a great finish. It has a bit of everything. There are some holes where it is better to hit an iron off the tee. In other places you need a lot of length.

In the quarter-final I beat Corey Pavin two and one, and in the semi-final Greg Norman two and one. The final was an epic battle with Seve, which he won two and one. I had inadvertently raised the tension for the match in a press interview the day before by saying that Seve intimidated his opponents on the course. I had not meant to say he was deliberately intimidating people, but the press made a lot of it.

Seve is such a competitive person that on the course he is totally focused on his own game. He can be very critical of his caddie, who is often his own brother. He rarely comments on a playing partner's good shot. He is never shy of calling the referee to get the best possible interpretation of rules. On top of that he is simply one of the best players ever to play the game. All this can be intimidating for his playing partners.

After the match when I was called into the press tent for interviews, Seve was still there and, perhaps goaded by the press, he challenged me publicly about what I had meant by my comment that he tried to intimidate players on the golf course. I replied quietly that I had not meant to say that and there was no need for us to have an argument. This seemed to defuse the tension.

In 1985 my form went from strength to strength. I won twice in the USA, twice in Europe and also in Australia and South Africa. The victory in the Australian Masters at Huntingdale was helped by a hole in one at the twelfth in the final round.

I have had eleven holes in one in my career, but only two in tournament play, the second being in the Volvo Masters in Montecastillo. The other holes in one were in practice rounds or with friends. I also had two holes in one in the par-three competition at the US Masters. Once at Sun City, when there was a big prize for a hole in one, my ball lipped out.

I won the Panasonic European Open at Sunningdale but did not play like a champion all the way round. At the second hole on the old course, I pushed my shot into the heather, short and right of the green. I was feeling cross with myself, thinking heather is horrible stuff and why did I hit it there?

When I got there the ball was sitting right on top of the heather! I was delighted – all I had to do was to chip it onto the green and hopefully hole the putt for par.

I addressed the ball but swung right under it. The ball moved an inch or two straight down but was still sitting on top of the heather. I stepped away, had a practice swing and then addressed the ball again. I did the same thing again. I swung right under the ball, even lower this time. So there I was, lying four but hadn't touched the ball since my second shot! Next time I got it out and made six or seven but still went on to win the tournament.

I also won the German Open in 1985 at Club zur Vahr, Earstedt, by seven shots from Michael McLean and Mark McNulty. My scores were 61, 60 and 62. However, play was rained off on the first day and the course was still flooded on the second day. They decided to reduce the length of the course by almost a mile so the scores do not count in the official records.

The big win that year was the US Masters, which is described elsewhere in this book. The following week I won the Heritage at Harbour Town. With three rounds in the 60s I took a one-stroke lead into the final round. In the final round I shot 70 but Bobby Wadkins tied me with a 68 to set up a play-off. I won on the first hole of sudden death with a routine par after Wadkins bogeyed.

At the end of 1985 I won the Sun City Million Dollar Classic. Sun City was the biggest tournament I have ever won in terms of prize-money – I won $300,000. That was a lot of money at the time. It was very satisfying for me. I had wanted to play at Sun City in 1984 and had been disappointed not to be invited. After all I had topped the money list and won tournaments all over the place and yet did not get an invitation to play.

After I won the Masters in 1985, I suppose they had to invite me! All the major winners were invited. It was nice to go there for the first time and win it. Having won, I qualified automatically for the next year. It is a great golf course to play and one of my favourites.

In twelve months I had won seven tournaments in five different countries. I was ranked number one in the world and I had a beautiful young wife. Yet, still, there seemed to be something missing . . .

Chapter 5

The US Masters 1985

The Masters is unique among the majors in that it is always at the same golf course, the Augusta National. That the course was designed by Bobby Jones, a legend himself, makes Augusta even more special. However, the course has been altered many times since then and it seems that almost every year they make some change or other.

There are some special events during the week, such as the past champions' dinner on the Tuesday night. Only the past champions and the chairman of the club are invited, and the reigning champion pays for the dinner. It is always a very special evening and great to dine with Jack, Arnie, Byron Nelson, Tiger Woods and all the other great champions. There used also to be a foreign players' dinner. There are two separate locker rooms, one for champions and one for others. All these things make the Masters a bit special.

When you play in a tournament you usually get free tickets for your family and friends. At the Masters, up until two years ago you had to buy tickets. If you are a Masters champion you are invited back to play in the tournament every year for the rest of your life. For the other majors it is only ten years.

I don't think it is coincidence that I have won my two majors there. I really like the golf course. To play well at Augusta you need to hit precision irons, to have good distance control and a good short game. These are three things I think

I'm quite good at. Augusta is a tough golf course and inevitably you are going to miss some greens so you need to be able to chip well and play imaginative shots around the greens to give yourself the chance of saving par.

Again, I am usually good at course management – at thinking my way around the golf course – and that is very necessary in the Masters. You need to have worked out where to hit the ball and where not to hit it.

At Augusta it is necessary to draw the ball from the tee on a number of holes and that is something that comes naturally to me. However, one thing that does not suit me is the length of my tee shot. I could do with hitting the ball a little further.

Although many people may think of me as a poor putter, I do enjoy the fast greens and the challenge of putting at Augusta. However, I would say that some of the greens are not fair, or rather some parts of some greens. But everyone knows that and you just have to make sure that you don't hit the ball to the wrong side of the flag. Take a green like the fourteenth, which has a huge ridge and the pin is often four yards over the ridge. Let's say you hit a shot in and it rolls to the top of the ridge. If it goes over the top it will finish off stiff (that is, with the ball stopping right by the pin): a certain birdie. But a shot hit a fraction less hard may get to the top of the ridge, stop and roll back down and off the green, leaving you with a probable bogey. The difference between the ball that just went over the ridge and the one that rolled back is very tiny but may cost the player two shots. The same thing can happen on the ninth and there are several greens where, if you hit the ball to the wrong place, you have no shot.

Sometimes you can hit a worse approach shot and have an easier putt than if you had hit an almost perfect shot. For example, you are better to be forty feet short with an uphill putt than to be pin high but facing a six-footer downhill or across a slope.

When I was younger I was one of the longest hitters in Europe but that has changed as the equipment has changed and I have got older. Also the courses are getting longer. In 2002 alone they added 300 yards to the Augusta National course – on top of the distance added in previous years. As a result, Augusta is a totally different golf course from what it was ten to fifteen years ago.

In my opinion that plays into the hands of the likes of Tiger Woods, Phil Mickelson, John Daly or Davis Love, who can bomb the ball 300 yards or more every time. The difference this makes is whether you are hitting a nine iron or a four iron to the green. And that makes quite a difference to some of the tricky greens at Augusta, particularly when you are hitting off a downhill or sidehill lie, and there are many of them at Augusta National.

The thirteenth and fifteenth are two of my favourite holes. If you hit a good tee shot, you have a chance of going for the green, but over the water. If you hit a bad tee shot then the decision is made: you cannot go for the green. But even if you can go for the green, you do not have to. It partly depends on the shot you are facing and partly on the state of the tournament.

For example, if you are leading by four shots, why take the risk? In those circumstances, I would lay up and leave myself a wedge. However, if you are one or two behind, you are going to have to go for it, as you may not have a better chance to make those shots up. But that is part of the fascination of golf. If you hit a good shot and carry the water, you can get birdie or even eagle. But if you put the ball in the water, you can easily finish up with a seven or an eight.

Another unique feature of the Masters is the par-three competition. This is part of the tradition. It is great fun for the spectators but, in all honesty, pretty meaningless for the players. The par-three course is a wonderful piece of property with flowers, trees and lakes. The greens are as good as on the main course and the atmosphere is amazing. It is like a zoo; there are so many people standing on top of each other around the holes!

Apparently, the winner of the par-three competition has never won the Masters. So if you are superstitious, you don't want to win the par-three competition in case that means you can't win the main tournament. I am not superstitious but I always look at it as a time to have fun rather than as a tournament to win. It is more about entertaining the crowd. For example, the three players might tee off at the same time so that there are three balls in the air at the same time. When I get to the green I might ask a little kid to take my putt and make his day, without worrying if it goes in or not.

As I said earlier, as a Masters champion I get an invite for life. Sam Snead and Gene Sarazen have sometimes teed off and even played a few holes. With my back, somehow I don't think that I will be playing in the Masters when I am ninety!

My first experience of the Masters was in 1982. The first thing that struck me was that I had never seen greens like that before in my life – even though I had played golf around the world I had never encountered such fast and tricky greens.

I finished eleven shots behind the leader and with the ten-shot rule I only missed the cut by one. I played thirty-six holes and had eleven three-putts in all – that is virtually one three-putt every three holes. Of course, you cannot three-putt eleven times and expect to stay in contention. The good news is that I learnt from that experience and when I won, three years later, I had only one three-putt in seventy-two holes.

In 1984 Ben Crenshaw won the Masters. I was thirty-first with 73, 70, 74 and 72, to finish twelve shots behind. I was about fifteenth after two rounds but went backwards from there. Still, it was progress to make the cut and play all four rounds.

I started the 1985 Masters with a 72 against Gary Hallberg's 68. A second-round 74 left me six behind Craig Stadler. I had dinner after the second round with a German journalist, Harry Valerian. He remarked that I must be pleased with my performance, as a reasonable finish would ensure a place in the top twenty-four and an invitation back next year. I surprised him by replying, 'Actually Harry, I am aiming to win this tournament.'

I did something very unusual that day too: I changed clubs halfway through the tournament. I wanted to hit the ball a little higher so I changed my irons for the third round.

On the third round I took a gamble and it paid off. On the thirteenth hole I had driven too far right. I was 225 yards from the green and had the small matter of Rae's Creek to negotiate. A good shot with my three wood at that time would carry 230 yards so there was no margin for error. I contemplated the shot and decided that if I was going to win the Masters, I had to go for it. It was not the best three wood I have hit. It was a little thin and low. It bounced short of the water, shot up in the air to clear it first bounce. It came to rest twenty feet from the hole. When I holed the putt for eagle, they wrote down '3' on the card. As they say, it is not how but how many! My gamble had come off.

At the end of the third round Ray Floyd led on four under par. Curtis Strange was second on three under, with Seve and me joint third on two under. It had been an interesting tournament for Curtis. He experienced everything that golf can throw at you in one week. He started with an 80 and was ready to check out of his hotel and go home. A 65 in the second round changed all that, and 68 in the third round suddenly put him one shot off the lead. That is the fascination of golf!

The playing order for the final day had me in the second last group with Seve. Curtis and Ray Floyd were in the last group. I had played very steadily all week and knew I had a chance. On the Sunday I did something quite unusual – I decided I wasn't going to look at the leader-board, just play my own game, play as well as I could and see what happened. Sometimes you can look at a leader-board and get depressed because you are too far behind. Other times you can see yourself two shots ahead and be too excited and lose your concentration.

Most of the time I look but I did have a stretch where I played well while not looking at the leader-board. When you think about it, most of the time you don't need to know. But equally you don't want to make the mistake Parnevik made at Turnberry in the Open Championship in 1994, when he didn't know the score and thought he needed to make birdie when he only needed par. He was too aggressive and made bogey. At the same time if you look at the board every hole, you can be so taken up with the scores that you cannot play your own game.

I took six on the second after being in two bunkers but holed from twelve feet for birdie on the third and from sixteen feet on the fifth. I just missed a good birdie chance on the seventh. So I came to the ninth hole, level for the day. I just glanced quickly at the board as I walked to the tenth tee. I couldn't believe it. I started the day two behind and hoped that I might have closed the gap a little – but I found that I was four behind.

I was getting sick and tired of good finishes – second or third – but not winning. I went into the back nine thinking, 'I am going to go for every flag.' I got par at the tenth – it is a difficult hole and a par feels like a birdie – and also parred the eleventh.

The twelfth hole is the par-three over water and even Jack Nicklaus says, when the pin is on the right, you don't go for the pin, you play over the bunker. It leaves you a longer putt but if you mis-hit it slightly, you finish up in the bunker and still have an up-and-down to save par. If you go for the pin and under-hit it, you are in the water.

On this occasion, the pin was back right and I went for it

and made birdie. I just kept on shot after shot, attacking every pin – shots that I normally might not have gone for. I got birdies on the thirteenth, fifteenth and seventeenth, and pars on the fourteenth and sixteenth.

I had played the tenth to seventeenth holes in five under. At the same holes Curtis was feeling the pressure. He three-putted the tenth, but then birdied the twelfth. On the thirteenth he hit his second into the creek, decided to play it as it lay and took two to get out. He found water and dropped a shot again on the fifteenth. With my birdie on the fifteenth, I had taken the lead by one from Curtis, two from Seve. The birdie on the seventeenth gave me a two-shot lead on the field.

As I came to the eighteenth I just needed a par for the tournament, barring miracles. I hit a one iron off the tee and a four iron to the green. It found the right bunker but was lying well. I played a good bunker shot to six feet. I read the putt as left lip but it did not break and missed left. I tapped in for my second bogey of the day. Curtis was coming up the eighteenth, needing a birdie for a play-off. In fact he made bogey and I won by two.

But it was an odd feeling as I watched him play the eighteenth on a TV in the scorer's tent. Half of me was wanting to celebrate but the other half of me kept telling myself to keep focused, as Curtis could easily make birdie and then I would have to play again. When I saw him hit his third shot the relief was incredible. I hugged Vikki. I was Masters champion!

The final positions were: Langer 68 for 282; Strange 71, Floyd 72 and Ballesteros 70 shared second place on 284.

When the Masters is over, they don't take you to meet the press but instead you immediately do a live TV interview in the Butler Cabin. They give you the green jacket – the traditional winner's prize – and ask you a few questions. They took me into the cabin and I think it was Jim Nance who asked me, 'Did you look at the leader-board? Did you know what was going on in the tournament?'

I replied, 'I was trying not to look but I saw it for the first time at the ninth and I thought, "Jesus Christ, I am playing well and I am four shots behind!" ' I just said it like that. I didn't mean anything by it. I wasn't a Christian at the time and I just said 'Jesus Christ' without thinking – it was just an expression of surprise that everyone used. Don't forget too that English isn't my first language and that in those days my English was a lot worse than it is now.

Now, as a Christian, I would see it as being disrespectful to the name of God, but at that time without thinking I just said it on national television. When I got home, I was amazed at the reaction. I received letters from a lot of people saying that I had offended them, I should think twice before using the name of God so casually, and so on.

I felt bad because it was just an expression to me and I certainly didn't want to offend anyone. While I wasn't a Christian myself, I had grown up going to church and would never have wanted to offend Christians.

My preparations for the Masters win had been thorough in all but one respect – my wardrobe! It was perhaps not the best day to wear red trousers and a red shirt. When the previous year's champion, Ben Crenshaw, put the green jacket on me, someone said that I looked like a Christmas tree!

Willi Hoffmann, my coach, had come over from Germany for the Masters but had to leave before the end of the final round to be back at work on Monday. Willi was literally on the plane home, waiting for take-off, when the captain announced that I had won. Somehow, Willi persuaded them to let him get off the plane and come back to join the celebrations. As Willi had shaped my game during the past nine years I was delighted that he was able to be with us.

Afterwards Vikki and I had dinner at the Augusta National Club with all the members, as tradition requires. Then we visited two Australians before heading back to where we were staying. I had met Frank Williams and David Inglis when I played in the Australian Masters, which they run, earlier that year. They had had a bet on me to win the Masters. They had staked $3,000. When I won they cleaned up about $100,000 – not much less than I made for winning the tournament.

As you can imagine they were having quite a party when Vikki and I turned up. We stayed with them for an hour or two. I reckoned they owed me a drink at least!

We went to bed but I had difficulty sleeping, I was too excited. I was up early next morning and bought all the papers to convince myself that it had really happened!

Up to that point, my career had been one of steady progress: getting on the tour, winning for the first time, being top of the European money list, making the Ryder Cup team and now, winning a major. Everyone told me that if you were a major winner then that would be the greatest thing, and it was – it was a thrilling event and I was very happy. But it wasn't what I thought it would be and there was still something missing, a feeling of emptiness.

I thought I had achieved everything, even more than I could ever have dreamed of. I had all the money I needed and a beautiful young wife – I had everything! And yet it wasn't enough. It was like, 'Well, where do we go now?' I didn't have real peace. It was as if there was still something missing. I always thought that if you win this tournament, or that tournament, if you made that much money then that's gotta be it. You're gonna feel wonderful. I felt good but I didn't feel wonderful.

I had achieved another of the milestones I had set myself. Great commercial opportunities would open up to me. But underneath it all there was a nagging question – is that it? Is that all there is? I had scaled the mountain but somehow the summit did not seem as exciting when I reached it as I had expected. There was an emptiness within me, saying there must be more to life than this.

I was very friendly with Bobby Clampett at that time and still am. Bobby is best known to readers in the UK for his great attempt to win the Open Championship in 1982. The Tuesday of the next week I played a practice round at Hilton Head with Bobby and must have shared some of this with him because he said to me, 'Why don't you come with us to the tour Bible study tomorrow night?'

I said, 'What is that?'

And he explained, 'A group of players and wives just meet for an hour and we read the Bible and pray together.'

I had grown up as a Roman Catholic, so I knew about God and felt comfortable with the idea, so I said, 'Sure, I'll come along.'

I also wanted to know more. As an altar boy in the Catholic Church, I had seen the priest with the Bible but I had never had my own. I figured I had it all together; I believed in God and hoped I would get to heaven. As I got more and more successful, I didn't need God. It was easy with a lifestyle like mine to get all wrapped up in things like cars, houses, position in the world rankings, the money list and so on. It seemed easy to be greedy, jealous and full of myself.

My priorities were golf, golf, and more golf; then myself, and finally a little time with my wife. Every now and then I prayed, but if my golf game was not good, my whole life was miserable, and I made everyone around me miserable.

I always thought just being a good person and keeping the commandments would hopefully get me to heaven. I didn't steal or kill and I tried not to hurt anyone on purpose. But as I got more and more successful, I thought I could do it all myself.

The leader of the study, Larry Moody, was speaking from John, chapter 3. Jesus told Nicodemus that he had to be born again. I had never heard this before, but it was exactly the message I needed to hear. Larry went on to explain what it meant in practical terms. I was amazed to realise that the only way to have eternal life was through Jesus Christ – that he died for our sins. And that it was not through worthy deeds or good behaviour that one received eternal life, because we can never live up to God's standard. We will always fall short.

I talked to Larry again. I had a lot of questions. I got my own Bible and read sections of it. After a period of time I began to realise that I had to make a choice. As I understood that God loved me so much that he sent his only Son to die for my sins, it was natural for me to ask the Lord into my life. Basically I just had to trust in him to forgive my sins. I had to make him the number one priority in my life, do everything to please him and not try to do it all myself. That hasn't always been easy. At times it has been very difficult because I still have a sinful nature. An extra problem is that the standards of the modern world, where achievement is all, are a lot different from what they are supposed to be.

Jesus said, 'I am the way, the truth and the life and no one gets to the Father but through me.' If you realise what this means you've got to stop, think about it for a second and then turn around and really focus on what you are doing in this world. No one in this world is good enough to get to heaven by their own deeds, but at the same time no one is bad enough that they couldn't be saved by Jesus Christ. When I realised that Jesus had died on the cross for my sins, for everybody's sins and I had to give over my life to him, I just recognised that this is the most important step or most important decision that I would ever have to take.

Jesus Christ stopped me in my tracks with his words, 'You must be reborn to enter the kingdom of God.' Since that day in 1985, my faith has played a big part in my life. It puts my priorities in a different order. Before I became a Christian my priorities were all about me and doing well on the golf course.

Now my first priority is pleasing God, second is my family and golf only third. I believe when your priorities are right, everything is managed better. Obviously at certain times, like when I am playing a tournament, golf is in a sense number one but overall I try to keep things in perspective so that golf is in its proper place in my life. I think I have been able to work out the right balance of time in my life and try to give sufficient time to the family and not let golf become dominant.

Some people say Christianity is a crutch for the weak. I think that is definitely wrong. I regard myself as a strong person but I need God in my life. Christianity is just a way of life that leads to eternal life with God in heaven and whether you are weak or strong or whether you feel you are fortunate or unfortunate has nothing to do with eternal life at all.

My wife, Vikki, felt the same, and she also accepted Christ as her Saviour. Since then, I have seen tremendous changes in her life, my own life, our relationship as husband and wife, and the way we treat our friends and others in this world. It was a life-changing week at Hilton Head and, by the way, I also won the golf tournament, the Sea Pines Heritage Classic.

Chapter 6

The majors

If you had the energy you could play a golf tournament almost every week of the year. However, only four of the tournaments have the status of being a major – the US Masters, the US Open, the Open Championship and the USPGA Championship.

The Open Championship has all the history and tradition in the world, going back to 1860 when eight players competed over three rounds of the twelve-hole Prestwick Golf Club in Scotland. Always played on a seaside course, the Open Championship would claim the strongest and most representative field of any tournament in the world.

The United States Golf Association was founded in 1894 and the US Open was first held the following year. The first US Open was a thirty-six-hole one-day affair, considered second in importance to the US Amateur Championship, which was held over three days the same week.

The USPGA is the fourth major both in the golfing calendar and, in most people's judgment, in importance. It was established in 1916 as the championship of the United States Professional Golfers' Association, which had been founded the same year. Until 1957 it had a matchplay format, but since then it has become stroke play.

The other major, the US Masters, has a special place in my career and is described in a separate chapter.

The majors are special because people make them important. Everyone says that these are the majors, and that these are
the tournaments that everyone wants to win. So when you win
a major it means more than anything else. Second, the golf
courses are set up harder for the majors. It is very demanding.
All the top players from around the world are there, and there
are not many tournaments where that is true.

If my career ended tomorrow, I would be very thankful for
what I have been able to achieve. My only big disappointment
is that I have never won the Open Championship. It is a
tournament with so much tradition, going back over 140 years.
The Open is the only major that takes place in Europe.

The Open Championship is always at a seaside or links
course. Generally I like links golf but I have had some
heartbreaking things happen to me. You have to accept that
links golf is not always fair. You are going to get bounces that
you don't deserve. It is a different type of golf and a very
natural way to play. I like the challenge of the wind and the
terrain. I like the mental challenge of deciding what is the best
way to approach each hole. But you must not expect it to be
fair. You can hit an excellent shot only to see it hit a slope or a
bump and go well off-line. Sometimes the bunkers are so deep
that it is virtually impossible to play out of them, without going
backwards.

It cannot be denied that I have had my chances to win. I
first played in the Open Championship in 1976 at Royal
Birkdale but missed the cut with rounds of 82 and 79. To play
in the Open was a massive step up for me. I missed the cut
again in 1978 at St Andrews, with rounds of 78 and 73. In my
third appearance, I played all four rounds in 1980, finishing
fifty-first. Not great but, as my first cut made in a major, it was
another milestone. In 1981 I was second behind Bill Rogers at
Sandwich. If you finish second you must have been in with a
chance of winning but, in all honesty, I probably wasn't ready
to win a major. I was a little too young and inexperienced to

win, even though I played well. I probably didn't quite believe that I could do it.

In 1984 at St Andrews I finished equal second. I like St Andrews. If you avoid the fairway bunkers there is plenty of room to drive the ball. If you drive well, you get the bonus of a better angle into the green.

I also like the choice of shots available if you miss a green. You can normally play anything from a six iron bump and run to a high sand iron. I like that. The greens too are pretty good, although I did once have a putt of eighty yards on one of the double greens. It is a very difficult shot as it isn't one you practise.

In 1984 with rounds of 71, 68 and 68, I entered the final day two behind Tom Watson and equal with Seve. Watson fell away on the Sunday with a 73.

I played with Seve in the final round. It came down to almost a matchplay duel between us. I played great golf but just could not buy a putt. I outplayed him from tee to green but he beat me by two shots because he holed the putts and I didn't. In the end I finished with a 71 to Seve's 69 – so near and yet so far. If I had putted even halfway decently, I would have won by two or three shots. The putter is the most important club in the bag.

In 1985 it was the same story. With rounds of 72, 69 and 68, I was sharing the lead with David Graham and was three clear of the field. I missed a short putt on the first, then got terrible breaks at two or three of the early holes, and the whole day was just a struggle. I shot 75 and lost by two. I could have shot two over par and won, but finished five over for the round.

I was once asked, if I could replay one shot from my career, which one it would be. I replied that it would be the first putt on the first hole in the last round at the 1985 Open Championship. I'd hole it and go on and win. I was only half joking.

Missing that shortish putt – about four feet – unsettled me a bit. Then I had a few bad bounces – something that can happen so easily at Sandwich. For example, on the fourth hole, a 470-yard par-four, I hit a great one iron just to the left side of the green, the perfect place for the ball to feed down towards the flag. But it hit a marshal on the foot and kicked the other way.

Then, at the next, I hit a good shot, which just rolled off the green, down the bank and into a terrible lie in the rough. Things like that happened three or four times. Usually these things even themselves out, but that day they went against me most of the time.

By the time I came to play the last hole I needed a birdie to tie Sandy Lyle and force a play-off. My approach was a little strong and right of the flag. I went through the green into the long grass. I hit the shot as well as I could and as I watched it, it seemed dead on line. In the end it grazed the hole and finished a few feet past. Not that it really mattered, I missed the putt.

I almost got into trouble that day. I picked up a sweater in the morning with the usual small Hugo Boss logo on the front. What I had not realised was that it also had BOSS in enormous letters on the back. Apparently the TV cameramen were struggling all day to get shots of me without catching the back of the sweater! The issue was that the rules specify that a sponsor's logo must not be bigger than a certain size.

Over the years I have been associated with a host of sponsors including Lufthansa, Hugo Boss, Linde, American Express, Ebel, Jaguar and Lacoste. I was once offered a contract by a dog-food firm. I declined it as I don't have a dog, although there have been a few occasions that I have played like one!

Looking back it would have been relatively easy for me to have won the Open Championship in either 1984 or 1985. If Greg Norman effectively won the Open in 1986 at Turnberry with his magnificent second-round 63, I threw away any chance I had with a third-round 76. I finished third, six shots behind Greg. However, I had a far greater victory that week with the birth of our first child, a baby girl we named Jackie. As I had a chance of winning the tournament, Vikki entered into a conspiracy to keep it from me and she went into hospital without me knowing.

In 1993 the Open Championship was back at Sandwich – rapidly becoming my favourite Open venue – and, again, I was well placed. It is an interesting reflection on the conditions in 1993, and perhaps the development in the game, that Bill Rogers' winning score in 1981 was 276, Sandy Lyle's in 1985 (when the wind blew) was 282. In 1993, a score of 276 would not have got you in the top ten! The winning total was 267.

Opening with a 67, 66 and 70, I was one behind Nick Faldo and Corey Pavin and equal with Greg Norman. Nick and I shot 67 – but Greg ran away with it with a 64. Corey had 70. I didn't really do much wrong but if someone produces a round of six under on the final day, they deserve to win.

My next chance to win was in 2001 at Royal Lytham. I was co-leader going into the last round and played in the final match with David Duval, who went on to win. It was fun to be in contention. David played very well and got some breaks. In that round he played three or four shots that could have turned out quite differently.

I didn't quite play well enough and I really lost it on the par-fives. I was one over for the par-fives when I was looking for two under. That hurt my chances. Nevertheless, it was a good showing. I played pretty steadily for most of the week. It was fun being there but, equally, I saw it as another chance missed.

I have won the US Masters twice but have never really come close to the winning the other two US-based majors. The US Open has proved a hard tournament for Europeans to win – Tony Jacklin, in 1970, was the last European winner. I have been asked a hundred times why Europeans find it so difficult to do well in the US Open and I still don't really know the answer.

To play well in the US Open you need to drive straight and to hit it a long way. The course is set up with very narrow fairways and deep, punishing rough right next to the fairway. Part of the problem is that courses in Europe are not usually set up like this. We are not used to these conditions so a lot of us struggle with the rough. There are very few normal chip shots because, even if you miss the green by only a small margin, you are likely to be deep in the rough, really having to dig the ball out.

However, things are changing as European courses are becoming more and more Americanised, with narrower fairways and more rough. Perhaps that means European players will have better results in the US Open in years to come.

In 1987 I finished fourth behind Scott Simpson at Olympic Club, San Francisco. I had chances that year. I remember one shot where I hit a lemon on a tree and the ball just dropped down dead and I made bogey. Another day the ball would have missed the lemon and gone another hundred yards. I shot 69, 69, 73 and 72, but needed four 69s to win and couldn't quite manage it.

The previous year, when Ray Floyd won at Shinnecock Hills, I played pretty well and was eighth. I had chances to win but I just didn't get up and down often enough when I missed the greens, and also I didn't hole enough putts. Over the years I have just missed too many fairways and collected too many bogeys. To win the US Open you have to do two things – you have to drive the ball well and you have to putt well. And I hadn't managed to do that consistently, four days in a row.

The fourth major, the USPGA Championship, changes course every year and the set-ups are a little different. It is often set up quite similarly to the US Open but at other times they make it a lot more open, more accessible and not quite as punishing. Perhaps more than the other majors it varies according to which course it is at.

I have never come close to winning the USPGA, never even finishing in the top twenty. For me part of the problem of playing the USPGA is that in August I am based in Europe. So you fly in on Sunday or Monday, you are fighting jet-lag and have been used to playing quite different golf courses. To have a real chance of winning you would need to have been there for a week or two. When you are competing with the best 150 players in the world it comes down to very small differences, and if you are tired or you are not used to that sort of course, that can be enough to keep you out of contention.

Compare that with the Masters in April. I am always in the USA in March and April, so it is much easier for me to be ready to play well than if I am just flying in for the tournament. Perhaps now that I am living in the USA, it will be easier.

As I approach the autumn of my career, I still have hopes of winning another major, ideally the Open Championship. Perhaps I want it too much and try too hard and my game slips because I am putting too much pressure on myself. Perhaps I am a bit like Lendl, who won everything but never Wimbledon!

Chapter 7

The Ryder Cup

The Ryder Cup is a three-day competition between twelve golfers from the USA and twelve from Europe. The match takes place every two years, alternating between Europe and the USA. Named after Samuel Ryder who presented the first trophy in the 1920s, it has a long tradition and an important place in the golfing calendar. On the first and second days there are four foursome matches and four four-ball matches. That means that only eight players on each team are involved at any one time. Then on the final day, the Sunday, there are twelve singles with everyone involved. That makes twenty-eight matches and, with one point awarded for each win, a team needs 14½ points to win the Ryder Cup.

It is a unique event for the players. There is so much hype about it – the build-up in the papers and golf magazines lasts for months so the interest is extremely high. With only twelve European players making the team, in a Ryder Cup year your priority is to make sure you are one of the twelve. The top-ten Europeans in the money list qualify automatically, with the captain being allowed to choose two other players.

Professional golfers are used to playing under pressure. Each week we have to make putts with lots of money at stake and with the eyes of the world upon us. What is different in the Ryder Cup is that you are playing not just for yourself but for your team and for your continent. When I made the team for my first Ryder Cup in 1981, I had very little experience of playing team golf. I was much more used to playing just for myself.

We're all hyped up and it's a problem. To treat it as just another tournament would be better. But with everyone around us being totally on edge, it's hard to stay calm and collected and it makes playing very difficult. It's a lot harder playing for your team than just playing for yourself.

I enjoy team golf very much but there is certainly an added pressure. When you play for yourself and make a mistake, it is only you who are the loser. In the Ryder Cup you have the added feeling of letting down your partner and the team – a completely different kind of pressure.

In most tournaments the spectators are neutral; they applaud the good shots and are quiet on the bad shots. But in the Ryder Cup the galleries are totally one-sided and will even applaud mistakes by the other team. So when we are playing in the USA it is a very odd experience for me to find a bunker or miss a putt, only to hear the crowd cheering. It is far more emotional than a normal tournament.

Foursomes (two players taking alternate shots with the same ball) is the most difficult form of golf. You only hit a shot about every ten minutes and it is hard to keep your rhythm going. Again you might not get to putt for three or four holes or to hit driver for a few holes. In four-balls each player plays their own ball with the best score of the four winning the hole. So if I mess up it doesn't matter as long as my partner delivers the goods. But in foursomes every shot counts and it all adds up to the most severe pressure I can think of in golf.

Apparently, I have one of the best records in the Ryder Cup foursomes. I cannot really think why that should be. I have played sixteen foursomes with eleven different partners, so it isn't even that we found a winning team and stuck with it. I don't think I've played with the same foursomes partner more than twice. Maybe it is because I am a steady player and, in foursomes, a par is often a good score; whereas in four-ball, with four good players shooting for the green, you have to expect that someone will make birdie.

On the subject of partnerships, some players have people they really like to play with. Europe has had great Swedish and Spanish pairs. I have always said to the captain, 'I don't mind who I play with – just put me where you need me.'

There are five series of matches and, a few times, I have played all five but that is extremely exhausting. Sometimes the morning can be slow, and if you are late in the order in the morning and the game goes to the eighteenth, but you are early in the order in the afternoon, you are virtually going straight from the eighteenth and onto the first tee again. As I have got older, I don't think that my body can cope with playing all five and I'm happy to sit one of them out.

My first Ryder Cup was in 1981 at Walton Heath. The USA had a very strong team and won easily, 18½ to 9½. You have to remember, too, that at that time USA had not lost a Ryder Cup since 1957. It was a mountain for us to climb. My Ryder Cup debut was with Manúel Piñero against Larry Nelson and Lee Trevino, and we lost by one hole. I was shaking, really nervous. I think it is the same with 95 per cent of players making their debuts. It is not easy for a player to turn up and play his best golf in the first round of the Ryder Cup.

The problem was that most of us didn't feel we stood a chance. We'd been losing for twenty-five years in a row, they had a very strong team and our whole attitude was totally different. Nowadays the players have a much more positive approach. They know they have won as often as the Americans over the last fifteen years and they'll go in with an attitude of winning, not 'how much we are going to lose by'. I remember when we were trying to lose by only five points instead of ten.

In my first Ryder Cup I was in awe of people like Jack Nicklaus and Tom Watson. Later in my career, when I had played with all the best players in the world and beaten them as often as they had beaten me, I had a different view of them. But at the beginning I was very nervous and didn't really know what to expect. I would assess my performance as reasonable, but not great.

On the second day I was again paired with Manúel Piñero. We beat Ray Floyd and Hale Irwin in the four-balls, but lost to Nicklaus and Watson in the foursomes. It was great experience and in those two days I had come face-to-face with some of the greatest players of that era. I halved the singles with Bruce Lietzke. Overall the Americans played extremely well. In the singles, for example, Sandy Lyle was something like nine under, but lost to Tom Kite, who was about eleven under.

The 1983 Ryder Cup was at the PGA National at Palm Beach Gardens and was altogether a closer affair. I played all five matches and was paired with Nick Faldo each time. That was a really good week. I liked the golf course, my swing was good, I was happy with how I played, and Nick and I had a good partnership. We won three of our four matches.

That was the first year that I thought we could win the Ryder Cup. We went into the final day 8–8. I won my single against Gill Morgan but in the end we lost by the narrowest margin, 14½ to 13½. In fact, it all came down to the last match when Bernard Gallacher lost to Tom Watson on the seventeenth. And of course, when it is as close as that, there are always one or two matches that could have gone either way and made the difference.

But, as a team, we were excited. We felt that we had got a lot closer than most people expected. We had all but beaten them on their own territory. That confidence carried forward and we thought we would have a great chance at the Belfry in 1985.

In 1985 I played all five rounds, and had four different partners. My record was two wins, a defeat and two halves. I played very well that week, especially in the singles where I beat Hal Sutton, 5 and 4. I ended in quite a spectacular fashion by knocking it stiff on the fourteenth.

That week there was a good illustration of the special character of matchplay golf. In the four-balls, Sandy and I were one down on the eighteenth green to Craig Stadler and Curtis Strange. All Craig had to do was hole a two-foot putt. In all honesty, it was really a 'gimme'. Sandy and I were thinking, 'Let's give it to him and then we can go.' But then we said, 'We know we have lost but let him putt it.' Incredibly, he missed it – it lipped out – and we halved the match. That just proved that ridiculous things can happen and it is never over until it is over.

Up until then, I had never done very well at the Belfry, which has never been one of my favourite golf courses. It was great to play well, but the main thing was that the team played well. To be part of the team that won the Ryder Cup for the first time in twenty-eight years was fantastic. By contributing three points while playing with four different partners probably marked me out as a good team player. Europe won 16½ to 11½.

In 1987 we went to Muirfield Village, confident that we could go one better and beat the Americans on their home soil. Again I played all five matches. I really liked Muirfield Village, which reminded me a lot of Augusta. In the first-day foursomes, I played with Ken Brown and lost.

After the first two hours of play on the first morning, USA were three up in the top match, three up in the second, four up in the third and two up in the fourth. It was hardly the start we had planned. The next two hours were better and we managed to fight back sufficiently to finish the session 2–2.

I partnered Sandy Lyle in the next three rounds and won them all. Sandy and I played some of the best golf I have ever seen in my life. We both played well and combined brilliantly. I could hardly believe some of the shots Sandy played. He could hit the ball almost straight up in the air with a two iron and carry it 240 yards. Not many people can do that, and I am not one of them!

In the second-day four-balls against Larry Nelson and Lanny Wadkins, we came down the eighteenth one up. All four drives hit the fairway but mine was the longest. Larry Nelson played first and hit the green. Sandy also put his ball on the green and inside Nelson. Wadkins, a great player under pressure, had come off two birdies. His shot produced a great roar from the gallery so, without being able to see it, I knew it was close. I had 150 yards and it looked as though we needed a three for victory. I struck an eight iron well. It was on line, landed on the green and stopped next to the pin, inside of Lanny's ball – a gimme. The atmosphere was electrifying and there was incredible noise.

I remember that on the first day as we took the lead, the US crowd became very quiet. I guess there might have been 2,000 Europeans and 10,000 Americans, but it was the Europeans who were making all the noise. The US press were urging the spectators to get behind the team. Next day it was unbelievable; most of the US officials and players' wives were carrying flags, and chanting 'USA'. That was a strange experience, something I had never seen in any Ryder Cup. I felt it was a bit over the top.

It is funny how the draw can keep throwing two players together, and that week I played against Larry Nelson three times. My singles match with him was very tight. It see-sawed back and forth, but there was never much in it. We came to the eighteenth, level. We each had a putt of two and a half feet and we just looked at each other and said, 'Good, good', shook hands and walked off. Larry and I are friends and I think we both felt, 'I don't want to miss this putt but equally I don't really want you to miss yours.' While I did not realise it at the time, that half point took us to fourteen points and meant that, even if we had not yet won, we could not lose.

It is, again, all part of the mystique of the Ryder Cup. Even in the most competitive situation imaginable you don't want your opponent – who may well be a friend – to lose a match by missing a putt and have to live with that for the rest of his career. I have played a lot on the US tour and quite a few of the US players are personal friends, so there is no animosity among us. It means that while I don't want to lose to them, I do want to beat them fair and square and not in controversial circumstances.

In 1989 the match ended 14–14 so we retained the Ryder Cup. However, it was a disappointing week for me. I played three and lost three and never really found my game. I just didn't have the confidence. Usually I played four or five times, but only three that week. I think I told the captain to leave me out as I felt I wasn't playing well.

There were some things that week that I didn't like and that, sadly, have got worse since then. I didn't like to see the gallery cheering when a US player hit his ball into the water. In my opinion that has no place in golf. When the Americans drove into the water, it helped my team, but that still didn't make me want to cheer. At no other tournament would you see the crowd cheering when someone's ball goes in the water.

My wife, Vikki, is American and the Ryder Cup is not an easy week for her. Sometimes in our team room there may be bad talk about the US team or the US crowd, and that must hurt her a bit. Vikki is proud of her country, and having to listen to people bad-mouthing your country is not a nice experience.

For the first few years it was a bit difficult as she had never been in that position before. She was certainly pulling for the Europeans but also wanted the best team to win. As time passed it became easier. Sometimes she finds the opening ceremony strange. When she sees the US flag – her flag – she has to remember that for this week it isn't her flag. It is the same if she hears 'The star-spangled banner'; but she has learned to see it as a golf tournament, not a matter of life and death.

One thing that was different about the 1989 Ryder Cup was that we held a Christian service on the Sunday morning behind the ninth and eighteenth greens. The idea arose from a conversation I had with Bruce Gillingham who, at that time, was leading the Bible study on the European tour. I asked the PGA and they said we could do it. I was the only European player who attended but there were several Americans. Chris de Burgh was staying in the hotel and he came and sang at the service, so we had wonderful music. There was quite a congregation too, as several hundred spectators had arrived early to reserve their places behind the two greens, where so much drama would unfold later in the day.

The 1991 Ryder Cup was at Kiawah Island. This was one of the worst Ryder Cups, in terms of attitude between players and the hostility of the US crowd. Some US newspapers called it 'the war on the shore'. I was very unhappy with that. It is not a war; it is a game. Corey Pavin got some criticism for stirring up the crowd and for wearing a military jacket. Paul Azinger and Seve had a big argument about a ruling and were shouting at each other.

My feeling is that none of that stuff should happen. There are officials who should decide what is right and wrong. You should play in a competitive way but in the spirit of the game too. I felt it got out of hand and the spectators got very rowdy. It was all over the top.

I played foursomes on the first day with Mark James, but lost to Ray Floyd and Fred Couples. Next day Colin Montgomerie and I beat Steve Pate and Corey Pavin. In the singles the captain put me in the anchor position, which meant I was the last player out on the course. My opponent was the double US Open Champion, Hale Irwin. As holders of the Ryder Cup, Europe only needed to draw to retain the trophy. However, the US team had a one-point lead with only my match on the course. I had to win.

I was two down after fifteen holes. I won the sixteenth and the seventeenth. It all came down to the last putt of the last hole in the last match on the last day. On the eighteenth, I was on the green in two. I had a long putt. I hit it just too hard and it went past the hole. So I could see what the ball did on this side of the hole and therefore what it was likely to do on my next putt.

Hale hit his putt, and it came up a few feet short. I conceded the putt, leaving me needing to hole a six-footer to win the match. Afterwards a lot of my colleagues asked me why I had given him the putt. They said that as Hale was really struggling over the last few holes, there must have been a chance he would have missed the putt. I said I just thought it was the right thing to do. I didn't want him to lose it, I wanted to win it. I wouldn't have conceded it if I had thought it was long enough for me reasonably to ask him to putt it.

I was putting well. I had made three or four putts longer than the one on the eighteenth. Over the back nine holes, I made a lot of crunch putts of six to ten feet. I made good putts on the fourteenth, fifteenth, sixteenth and seventeenth, so I was confident.

I was sure that the putt would move slightly. I always read putts with Peter and as I lined it up, I said to him, 'Where do you see it?'

He said, 'Left edge.'

I agreed with him. The problem was that there were two spike marks directly on the line, about halfway to the hole. And on the Bermuda grass, they get very crusty and crunchy – unlike the soft bent grass that we are used to in Europe.

I said to Peter, 'What about these two spike marks? They are right on my line.'

He said, 'Yes, I see them.'

My concern was that if I hit the spike marks, the ball could go anywhere. We looked again and decided that if, instead of going left edge, as I wanted to, I hit the putt straight, and just missed the spike marks but hit it firm, it might not break but go straight in.

I prayed for courage, strength, and a quiet hand. When I hit the putt, I felt it was a good stroke. I thought I had made it but, of course, it rolled just barely past the hole.

There are photographs of me just after the putt has missed with a very pained expression on my face. It wasn't just because we had lost the Ryder Cup, though that was bad enough. Part of it was just that the putt had not gone in, after it had felt so good.

There has been so much speculation about why I missed the putt, the pressure of the occasion and so on. In fact I struck it well. I suppose it was a slight misread, possibly because of the spike marks.

I didn't mention the spike marks at the time. In fact I didn't tell anyone for years. I was afraid that if I had said that right away, they would have said it was just an excuse – he couldn't handle the pressure and he blames it on spike marks.

It was a chance a golfer only gets once in a lifetime, to hole a putt for the Ryder Cup. I did my best but in the end it was not good enough.

As I walked off the green, I felt bad for my team. I could handle that I had missed the putt and I might be blamed for it. But I didn't want the other guys to suffer. Then as I walked into the team room there was Seve giving me a hug and crying. He set me off.

At first I wanted to say, 'Don't cry, it's not that serious', but I guess, for some, it was. And of course some people are more emotional than others. So I felt bad for the captain and the team because it was such a crucial thing. But as I got my perspective in order, I got it into context.

Of course, I was very disappointed – for the team, all my

colleagues, the captain, for the whole tour, the continent, that I had let them down. I had missed a putt. On the other hand, I knew I had tried my best and had done everything I possibly could.

My relationship with God, with Jesus Christ, put it all in perspective. When I look back now I realise that there are far more important things in life than winning a tournament, or losing a tournament, or making or not making a putt. I know I did my best and I can live with it and go on. I don't live in the past. I live in the future. I am amazed that over ten years later, people still want to talk about the putt.

When a journalist asked me about it the following week, I said, 'Looking at the Ryder Cup from a Christian point of view, there has only ever been one perfect man, the Lord Jesus, and we killed him. I only missed a putt.'

At the 1993 Ryder Cup at the Belfry, we had a Bible study on the Wednesday night, attended by six players and their wives. On the Sunday morning we repeated the service of four years earlier. About 400 people were present – many of whom had come early to reserve a good vantage point. The service had a transatlantic flavour, with Bible readings by Corey Pavin and me. The Rev. David Janzen – whose brother, Lee, was in the US team – took part in the service, along with the two tour chaplains, Bruce Gillingham (Europe) and Larry Moody (USA).

We were determined to regain the cup, which we had lost by the narrowest margin at Kiawah Island. I played in the first-day foursomes with Ian Woosnam and we beat Payne Stewart and Paul Azinger, 7 and 5. We played very well and they never really got it going. It was a great win.

I played two more matches, winning one and losing the other. Still we entered the last day one point ahead and with everything to play for.

I lost my singles to Tom Kite, 5 and 3. I played reasonably

well, but Tom played exceptionally well. An example of how he was playing and the confidence he had was at the tenth hole, where you have to cross water to reach the green. He was two up but he took a three wood and hit it to ten feet. It never seemed to cross his mind to lay up. When you are two up, you could, say, hit a seven iron and a pitching wedge and not lose the hole. He was so on form that he took the shot on and pulled it off. He was way under par and I wasn't playing well enough to match him. The Americans rather ran away with it that Sunday, winning 15–13.

In 1995 the Ryder Cup match was played at Oak Hill Country Club, Rochester, New York. I played all five rounds with three different partners and, by one of those freak draws, I was up against Corey Pavin four times, and the little terrier won three of them! I felt my game was just average that week, not brilliant. Corey played very well and deserved to win.

But it was a tremendous win for the team and that was what mattered most. The Americans were very confident, having won in England in 1993. So it was just great for us to go over there and beat them, particularly on a course that they felt would favour them. Europe won 14½ to 13½.

The 1997 Ryder Cup at Valderrama was a good week for me, and for Europe, as we won again, 14½ to 13½. I played three times on the first two days, always with Colin Montgomerie. On the first morning we lost the foursomes to Tiger Woods and Mark O'Meara. Neither Colin nor I played quite well enough. We played them again in the afternoon four-ball and beat them 5 and 3 – both playing a lot better – and were delighted with the result.

I played Brad Faxon in the singles, winning 2 and 1. As it turned out that was the deciding game and, after I had won, we could not be beaten. Of course, every point counts and it is the captain's decision whether you play early or late, but it is something extra when you find yourself in the decisive match.

The 1997 victory ranks as high as any. I feel that a Ryder Cup victory gives me as much pleasure as a major victory. The US team in 1997 was as strong as any I have seen but on the day, the European side was just a little better.

When Seve was appointed captain for the 1997 Ryder Cup, I fully supported the decision. He seemed the natural choice. He is so experienced and has the respect of all the players. With the match taking place in Spain, it seemed even more appropriate. It was great for him to be a winning captain in his own country. 1997 was my ninth Ryder Cup, having played every one since 1981.

As I did not win any tournaments in 1998 or 1999, it would be touch and go whether I finished in the top-ten automatic qualifiers for the team and in the end I finished fifteenth. It was down to whether or not the captain, Mark James, picked me. He did not.

Not making the 1999 Ryder Cup team was, without doubt, the most difficult moment in my golfing life. I have been disappointed not to win tournaments when I put myself in the winning position but then could not quite pull it off. This was much worse. Even if I was struggling to make the top ten, I expected to be one of the captain's two picks. What is more, everyone – my fellow professionals, caddies and golf writers – told me that I would be.

It seemed to be between Andrew Coltart, Robert Karlsson and myself, with people telling me that it had to be me. Jesper Parnevik was always going to be the other pick. The fact that they were all telling me that I would be on the team increased my expectations and, consequently, my disappointment. But the choice was Andrew Coltart.

While I did not play in 1999, I was saddened by what happened during the Ryder Cup competition. The way the

Americans ran across the green after Justin Leonard's putt was unacceptable. It wasn't the end of the match; José María Olazábal should have received the courtesy of an equal chance to hole his putt. It wasn't a good moment for golf.

If I had not made the top ten in 2001 I don't know if I would have been one of Sam Torrance's picks. The press seemed to think it would be Jesper Parnevik and Sergio García. I have no problem with Sergio – he had an exceptional year – but I think if you compare my record in 2001 with Jesper's, I had a very strong case for selection. To be fair to Sam, he admitted to me that he had a very difficult choice. He told me there were three players he really wanted on the team, all of whom might just miss out on qualifying. Fortunately, my victory in the Dutch Open as well as the third place in the Open Championship meant that I was comfortably in the top ten.

I was terribly disappointed that the Ryder Cup was cancelled but I am convinced it was the right decision. It would have been very hard for the Americans to leave home so soon after the events of 11 September.

In my nine Ryder Cups I have played under four captains. I was very satisfied with all my Ryder Cup captains and have nothing negative to say about any of them. The first one was John Jacobs. He is a very respected golf teacher and player. He is a real gentleman. I have a lot of respect for him. In 1981 I was really so much in awe of being in the team that a lot of it went over my head. However, I thought he did a good job as captain. The problem was that, at that time, the gulf between us and the Americans was pretty big. We didn't really have much of a chance of winning.

I enjoyed playing under Tony Jacklin. He was always very upbeat and positive. He really gave the team confidence and tried to make us believe that we could win. I think he did a great job. He deserves a lot of credit for engineering the wins in 1985 and 1987.

Bernard Gallacher also did a good job. He really took care of everyone. He was a good communicator and explained to the team exactly what he was trying to achieve. I felt very comfortable with the set-up under Bernard. He was very unfortunate in 1991 and 1993 to lose by narrow margins but I was really pleased for him that he had the satisfaction of winning in 1995. I felt that you could not have had a better captain than Bernard. I am sure he was under pressure but he never seemed to show it.

Seve Ballesteros was a different style of captain, but he too was very upbeat and very positive. He was very good at pep talks, really making us feel confident, helping us to believe that we were better than the Americans and that we could beat them. Having been such a great player and such a successful Ryder Cup player, Seve certainly had the respect of everyone.

As captain Seve was almost wanting to play the shots for us. Of course we had to play our own game but that is just Seve. He gets so involved. He does nothing by half measures. I think that the hardest thing for a captain – especially when you are still an active player – must be to have to watch the action and not to be able to take any part in it. Seve did well and certainly gave it everything he had.

The 2002 captain, Sam Torrance, did an excellent job. He involved everyone, consulted widely and was fun to be around. With his experience both as a player in eight Ryder Cups and of course as Mark James's right-hand man last time, he certainly knew what the Ryder Cup was all about. I have devoted a complete chapter to the 2002 Ryder Cup, new for this edition, which you will find near the end of the book.

If I were ever asked to be Ryder Cup captain, it would be a great honour and delight. It is something I would really like to do but, of course, it is not up to me. It is a big job but I think I could handle it. It starts months before the Ryder

Cup week. Dealing with the press in the build-up, during the week and after, is only one part of the job.

There are so many events to attend – press conferences, sponsors' events, meetings etc. Again, when the Ryder Cup captain plays in a tournament he is the centre of media attention, irrespective of how he plays.

While we are on that subject, I am not completely happy with the qualifying procedure for the Ryder Cup. At the moment the top-ten Europeans on the European tour qualify automatically, with the captain having two picks in addition. It has been the same system for at least ten years and it was probably all right to begin with, when all the top European players played only in Europe.

Now, there are ten to fifteen Europeans playing fairly regularly in the USA and, of course, these include some of the better players. What you want in the Ryder Cup is the twelve best European players, but the present selection procedure does not guarantee that. The system rewards a player who plays a lot of tournaments. If you play thirty-five tournaments on the European tour – but are just an average player – you are going to make more money than a really good player who only plays eleven tournaments.

To illustrate: player A plays thirty-five tournaments while player B plays eleven. Player A finishes £100 ahead of player B in the list and gets into the Ryder Cup team. But which of them is the better player? It is clear in my mind that the system is not fair. It is not right that you can play your way into the team just by playing a lot of tournaments.

I think the fairest way to choose the team would be to take the top-twelve European players in the world rankings. The world rankings has had its critics over the years, but it has changed and become more accurate and up-to-date. I think that now most players have confidence in it. I have heard suggestions of taking the top three in the European money list, the top-six Europeans from the world rankings and giving the

Enjoying tea with my parents Wally and Erwin.

With the other caddies at Augsburg Golf Club. I'm the smallest one, next to my brother Erwin on the far right.

In my Sunday best (aged 8). I was an altar boy at the local church.

Training for my 'mad ambition': to win a downhill ski race.

Vikki and me on one of our many skiing holidays with the children: Jackie, Stefan, Christina.

A more recent picture of me with my parents.

A recent family portrait (Vikki, Christina, me with Jason, Stefan, Jackie).

The famous tree-iron shot. I played it by the 17th green during the 1981
Benson & Hedges International at Fulford, York.

Goldilocks makes an appearance at the 1981 Ryder Cup.

Perhaps that's the answer to the putting problems – letting my brother Erwin do it!

Becoming a Bobby! (The European Open, 1985)

The US Masters 1985 – Ben Crenshaw helps me into the
coveted green jacket. With my red trousers someone quipped
that I looked like a Christmas tree!

captain three choices. That would be better than the current system, but I think that to simply take the top-twelve Europeans in the world rankings would be the fairest and easiest. The aim is to get the twelve best players and I think the world rankings would achieve that.

The reason I would use the world rankings is that every tournament counts – anywhere in the world. With the present system, only European tour events and the majors count. A player could win four significant tournaments in the USA but that would count for nothing in Ryder Cup terms. You would not be in the team even though you would clearly be one of the best players. I think that is wrong.

Having criticised our system, I am not sure that the Americans have got it right either. They give points only to the top ten. So you could finish eleventh in every tournament and end up with no Ryder Cup points!

As a German player, it is a disappointment to me that the Ryder Cup has never been played in Germany. I don't know everything about how the decisions are made, but it does seem as though money is a big factor and whoever puts up the most money is likely to get the Ryder Cup. Of course the golf course has to be of the right quality as well. I think it has been in England too many times and at the Belfry too many times. I am delighted that we are going to Ireland in 2006, but that should have happened years ago, and that the Ryder Cup is going back to Scotland.

I would certainly like to see the Ryder Cup go to the Continent more often. So far it has only been to Spain. Both Sweden and Germany have strong cases. Think how many excellent players Sweden has produced. Golf in Sweden is booming. In Germany we have three very big European tour events. It would be nice to see these countries rewarded for their contribution to the tour. But the decision has been taken that the Ryder Cup venue will not leave the British Isles again until after 2016.

I understand that tradition and history demand that the UK gets preferential treatment but I feel that to alternate between the UK and the Continent would be fairer and would recognise the growth of golf and the contribution to the tour made by continental Europe. Like so many things in life, it seems to be driven by money.

One thing I have always disagreed with is that the profits of the Ryder Cup are split between the European tour and the British PGA. That means that the German, Swedish, Irish, Spanish and other PGAs get nothing, despite the contribution of their players. When the Ryder Cup became a European event and not just a British event in 1979, there should have been an adjustment to the finances. I have expressed this opinion more than once but it is not up to me.

I am sometimes asked if we should choose a particular type of course that would serve the European team better. A few years ago I would have said that links golf would give us a better chance – windy and bouncy. However, I think things have changed and the modern US player is better at adapting to the conditions.

They all used to hit the ball very high and found the wind difficult. Partly due to the changes in the technology of golf, the top US players can now hit the low spinning ball as well as their traditional high shot. If links golf really would give the Europeans such an advantage, why aren't European players winning the Open Championship every year?

The Ryder Cup has been an important part of my career. I've cried in Ryder Cups, but I've had many laughs as well. When you play for a team and a country it just means that much more and it can be hugely emotional. When we won at the Belfry in 1985 and two years later at Muirfield Village, those were both very special to all of us. Then, on the negative side, there was Kiawah when I missed that putt.

It has been wonderful to see the Ryder Cup grow and develop into one of the biggest sports events in the world. That makes it even more important to uphold the strict etiquette and sportsmanship of the game of golf. We need to continue to respect the game of golf, respect each other and to enjoy the competition.

Chapter 8

Putting problems

So much has been written about my putting over the years that it would fill a few books on its own. However, I thought that in this book I should describe it as I see it. Popular opinion has it that I am a bad putter. One journalist once wrote: 'The greens here are so good that even Bernhard Langer did not three-putt them.'

There is no doubt that I have had my putting problems. However, you cannot win fifty golf tournaments if you cannot putt. The truth lies somewhere between the two extremes.

As I said, I have the label of being a bad putter. No matter what I do – even though for two years I have been top of the statistics as the best putter in Europe – the label sticks. Most of my career I have putted well but because of the problems I have had, I have this reputation, and people keep bringing it up. There is nothing I can do about it.

It is also true that I have had times when I have had real problems. At times my putting was so bad that people were coming to watch me, but in the manner of people who go to motor-racing to see a crash!

As an indication of how bad my putting was, I once four-putted from three feet. I was double-hitting the ball. In a matchplay situation, opponents refused to concede even one-foot putts to me as they could see that the chance I would miss it was greater than the chance I would make it.

As a boy, as a caddie and as a young pro I thought I was a very good putter. I had problems in 1976 in my first year on the European tour, down in Spain and Portugal. That was the first time in my life I had been exposed to very fast greens.

I developed 'the yips'. It is hard to describe the yips. It is the putter not doing what you want it to. It is an involuntary and uncontrollable movement of the muscles, resulting in a fast, jerky, uncontrolled putting stroke. It's like a muscle spasm; you hold the putter this way or that way – it doesn't matter; and sometimes you can't take it back. You freeze; you totally freeze – or you just jerk.

Your muscles do something and your hands feel as if they are not part of your body. It is a churning of the stomach, an extreme nervousness. It is a loss of nerve. Sometimes I did not know how to take the putter back and then, once I got it back, I didn't know how to take it through.

As I look back on that time, I realise I was not used to the lightning fast greens in Spain and Portugal where the first tournaments I played on the European tour in 1976 took place. Greens in Germany at that time tended to be very slow.

I did not have any money at that time so I was under a lot of pressure to perform. I knew that I had enough money to play only a certain number of tournaments and if I did not win some money, I would have to leave the tour and go back to being a club pro and to teaching. I wanted to prove to everyone out there that I was good enough. I put too much pressure on myself.

As a result of the pressure it all became too important. I was desperate to succeed, and the result was that I got the yips. They were with me on and off for the next few years and in 1978–79 it was terrible. There were many days when I wanted to quit and go back to teaching golf. The only thing that kept me going was the knowledge that I was a good ball-striker, and the belief that if I could improve my putting, I would be one of the best. As often as I thought about quitting, I would remind myself that the Langers are not quitters.

When the yips first struck, I received many pieces of advice on how to conquer them – new putter, different techniques, various superstitious rituals. I made dozens of technical adjustments and tried twenty different putters. There was no miracle cure. My putting gradually improved. I was not putting well enough to win a tournament but I was putting well enough to make the cut and some money. That old putter that I bought for £5 on Seve's advice during the Hennessey Cup helped me regain confidence and become a winner in 1980.

I putted well with that putter for a year or two and then in 1982 I had problems again. I was playing in a TV match, Men versus Women at Woburn. My putting was terrible but it wasn't the yips. I was decelerating every time I tried to strike the ball. To overcome this problem I changed my grip and started placing my left hand below my right. As I practised and got used to this new grip, I began to feel more comfortable with it. If there is a secret to putting, it is to feel comfortable over the ball. I still used a normal grip for longer putts.

I changed from a regular to a cross-handed grip, just to get away from the problem. It felt different and I was more relaxed. I putted like that for the next seven years and had arguably my greatest success with that approach.

I was ranked number one in the world for a short time and in the top three for several years. I was winning tournaments all over the world. Everything was going so well. Then in 1988 I got the yips again. I was leading a tournament after two rounds, I was ten under; and the next two days I shot five over and from that day on I had the yips again. They wouldn't go away and I had them for about five or six months. I went from the very top to the very bottom.

I could not see my way out of this. I was a believer by then and I prayed to God, 'Lord, I believe you have given me this talent to do well and to have a platform to speak up as a Christian and to share what I have been blessed with. But it looks as if you are taking it away again. Lord, if you want me to do something else, if you don't want me to play golf, tell me where you want me. Tell me what you want me to do and I'll do it because I am not having any fun out here at the moment.'

These were very trying times and often I asked the Lord, 'Why me? What have I done to deserve this?' Giving up golf was not at all what I wanted to do but I was ready to give up if I felt that was what God was telling me. I got through that period with lots of prayer, a change of grip and lots of hard work. It took a while but I came out the other side and started playing well again.

I was very fortunate that just before I would otherwise have given up, a friend of mine came over and spent a couple of days with me. He prayed with me and he said, 'Bernhard, I don't think God wants you anywhere else. You should just persevere and continue what you are doing and he will show you the way out of this. He wants you playing golf. He wants you to be a success at golf so that you can reach out to other people and hopefully be a good example to others.' I want to state here that it is only through my relationship with Jesus Christ that I have been able to endure such hard times and still remain so content.

I went from the cross-handed to what you might call the split cross-handed forearm grip, with my hand on the forearm. I just split up my hands, one on the club and one on the other arm, and leant the shaft against the forearm and held it very lightly. This way, one arm is totally relaxed and the other one holds it very lightly. But I felt it was a really good stroke for short putts because I took all the small muscles out of the stroke. I took the wrist out of it, basically. When you putt normally I would say you use about six joints – the two wrist joints, the elbows and the shoulder joints. With this putting grip, I was taking the wrist out of it and just focusing on the two shoulder joints.

In 1989 the Spanish Open was a very big win for me. I had struggled all year and was gradually coming back. I used the new grip. After going twelve months without a win and putting so badly, managing to keep it together and win was a massive boost to the confidence. It was set up with a 67 including only 27 putts on the last day.

I used that grip successfully for about another seven years. It is funny how it always seemed to be seven years. I cannot explain why my putting should remain solid for that long or why it should suddenly go pear-shaped.

Then I started having problems again. In 1996 I felt I needed to change again and I started using the long putter, which I have used ever since. Occasionally when I am playing with my son or someone, I might borrow a conventional putter and think, 'This feels nice – perhaps I'll start playing with it.' But I have never yet had the confidence to play a competitive round with a conventional putter. I am not under contract to use any particular putter so I can change whenever I want.

I can't really explain why I like the long putter. I suppose it has to do with feeling comfortable and not feeling the pressure. If you are not comfortable and not relaxed, you cannot putt. These days the standard is so high and the margins so tight that if you cannot putt, you cannot compete.

I seem to need less time practising with the long putter than I did with the short one. And it is easier on my back, which is also important, given the problems I have with that.

In 2001 I think I was eighth in putting in the USA, and that explains a lot of my success that year. Putting is half of the score so if you are putting well, you should be scoring well.

Sometimes in my heart of hearts I wish I could go back to the short putter. I think what would stop me using a short putter in the next tournament is the fear that I might yip again, which is a terrible feeling. I will probably never totally get rid of the fear of the yips coming back. As much as I want to forget it, the thought is always there. The yips is such a horrible thing that I wouldn't wish it on my worst enemy. In putting, as in all golf, as I said before, the bottom line is not how but how many.

I still practise putting quite a lot. At each tournament you have to get the feel and the speed of the greens. That is very important as we play at a different golf course each week and the speeds will vary. They may even vary from day to day during the same tournament. Then I also work on technique or feel or alignment. By technique I mean trying the ball in different positions, or making sure my eyes are in the right position or that my head is not moving. Even with putting I try to have the same pre-shot routine and to feel comfortable with that.

My approach to putting is to get the tempo, rhythm and speed right – to pick a spot and aim at it. There are a few fundamentals that are important to almost everyone, no matter what your grip is like. One of them, I believe, is that you have to be very comfortable when you are over the putt; when you address the ball you must be really relaxed, which means your weight has to be balanced on your feet and your arms should hang very relaxed and very loose. There should be hardly any grip pressure. Sometimes I see amateurs with white knuckles, which means they are very tense and very tight and as a result don't have a lot of feel.

The other thing I try to do is to keep my eyes over the ball because I believe that when I turn my head I can look down the line much better than if my eyes were way inside or way outside the golf ball. To check this you just let the putter drop, sort of hang from your eyes down, and it should be right over the ball.

Third, I think that the shoulder alignment and the feet alignment and knees and hips should be like a railway track, if you imagine the ball as one rail and the feet/shoulders as the inside rail. I like to have my shoulders aiming at the hole so that I can putt with my shoulder. I have learnt over the years that it is much better to use big muscles instead of small muscles. It's harder to jerk with the bigger muscles than with the fine muscles in your fingertips.

I have been through an awful lot with the putter but I've also been blessed tremendously. I've had the whole spectrum. I have known the good times and the bad times. More than twenty-six years after the putting problems first appeared, I am still playing golf at the highest level. I have come through the yips three times. Technique, hard work and character have played a part, but without the strength of the Lord, I would not have made it.

Chapter 9

Success and despair in the late 1980s

Having become a major winner in 1985, and been ranked number one in the world, I had just about fulfilled the last of my ambitions – except for winning the Open Championship. The challenge now was to try to stay at the top. However, form and confidence are mysterious concepts.

Sometimes, especially when I have played the previous week or two, I will go into a tournament feeling confident. I may think I like the way I'm swinging, and feel that I am putting well. I may like the week's golf course. But if I have come from two or three weeks of missing the cut, then I am probably not feeling comfortable with anything. My confidence is down and I go into the tournament not feeling great. Most of the time I have a sense of where my game is and how likely I am to be in contention.

When I have not played for two or three weeks, it is harder to know how I will play. Sometimes when I am warming up on the range, I hit terrible shots and think to myself, 'Goodness, what is going to happen today?' Then I go out on the course and finish up shooting four or five under. Other times, I hit the ball well on the range and then go out and shoot four or five over. It just doesn't make sense.

Good results breed confidence. Confidence breeds more confidence. Bad results send you in the opposite direction. It is very hard to say to yourself, 'I am the greatest player in the world' when you have missed three cuts in a row and just shot 80.

I know when I'm swinging well and when I am not – it just makes me feel confident over the ball. In golf, good and bad are very close together. With putting, there are days when you just know that you are striking the ball well and it is rolling perfectly. On other days you just feel awkward over the ball.

In 1986 I played a lot in the USA and, without winning a tournament, I did enough to finish tenth in the US money list. In Europe I played only seven tournaments, winning the German Open and tying for the Trophée Lancôme. I also had four third-place finishes.

I won the German Open at Hubbelrath Golf Club, Düsseldorf, but only just. That was an eventful week to say the least. On the Tuesday I was due to fly from America with El Al, the Israeli airline. Vikki, Jackie and I arrived to check in one and a half hours before take-off. To my surprise there was no one around. Why had they not started checking passengers in?

Eventually someone came to the desk and told us that El Al close the check-in two hours before take-off. We were too late. After a bit of persuasion he agreed to see if he could get us on the plane. The crew decided we could fly but were not sure about the luggage. I said, 'Come on, you have over an hour to get the luggage on the plane. What's the problem?'

We made the flight, but on arrival at Düsseldorf we found that not one of our eight pieces of luggage had arrived. It is inconvenient not to have your clothes but it is quite hard to play in a golf tournament without your clubs! I called my brother and asked him to get an old set of clubs to me immediately. I practised with them.

On Wednesday two pieces of luggage arrived – but not the clubs. By Thursday morning the clubs still hadn't arrived so I played the first round with old clubs that I was not really comfortable with. I opened with a three-over-par 75.

I had my clubs for the second round and shot 65. A third-round 66 should have put me in control but Rodger Davis shot a fourth round 64 to tie. I won the play-off.

In 1987 I again split my time between Europe and the USA. In the USA I was twenty-third in the money list. My best performance was second to Corey Pavin in the Bob Hope Classic.

In Europe I played only ten tournaments but still managed to finish fifth in the money list. I won two tournaments in a short period of time: the Whyte and Mackay PGA Championship at Wentworth, and the Carrolls Irish Open at Portmarnock.

I won the PGA by four from Seve and the Irish by ten from Sandy Lyle. All eight rounds were in the 60s and I finished eighteen and nineteen under respectively. It was just one of those periods when it all went right. I was swinging well, making few mistakes and the putts dropped. I tied with Sandy for the German Masters but lost the play-off on the second hole.

1988 was the most depressing year of my life. My career seemed to be going backwards. This was because of a further outbreak of my putting problems, as I describe elsewhere, and at the time I thought seriously about quitting. Yet I still felt that I had beaten the yips before and could beat them again.

The year started well when I won the first tournament. I had won a tournament in Europe every year since 1980 and managed to keep that going with a victory in the Epson Grand Prix, a matchplay tournament.

Matchplay tournaments are always a bit of a lottery. You can be the second-best player on a given day, but be knocked out if you happen to play the best player. My toughest match was my first. It was actually the second round as I had a bye in the first. I was two down to Bill Longmuir with three to play. I got it back to level and won at the nineteenth. I beat Tony

Johnstone two and one (two up and one to play). On the Sunday morning I beat Rodger Davis one up in the semi-final. I changed my putter before the final against Mark McNulty. It was a good decision as I started with three single putts in four holes and finished up winning four and three.

My second tournament in Europe was the PGA Championship at Wentworth. I opened with 67 and 66 but followed that with 74 and 73 when putting problems set in. In the Open Championship at Royal Lytham I took five putts from about five feet at the seventy-first on the way to an 80. I missed cuts at the Dunhill British Masters, the Irish Open and the European Open.

I finished the year thirtieth on the European money list and 111th on the American.

I missed three cuts in 1988, which brought to an end an amazing sequence; I had made fifty-four successive cuts since 1983. I just said to myself, 'You have got to keep going, keep working, keep trying.' You find out a lot about your character when you are in slump as bad as that. I found out a lot about myself then. Thankfully I got through the bad times.

In 1989 with my new putting style I began to recover the lost ground. While my new putting style looked odd to many people, as far as I was concerned it seemed to be working and that was what mattered. I was holing my share of twenty- and thirty-footers. One golf writer, John Hopkins, wrote, 'Wherever you looked this year, there was Langer using a wonky grip, a flat swing and an unusual putting style – and still winning tournaments.'

I won the Peugeot Open de España. A third round of 67 (with 27 putts) gave me a two-shot lead. However, with three holes to play I had lost the lead and was equal with Paul Carrigill. I holed a fifty-foot putt for birdie on the sixteenth, and on the par-three seventeenth I hit a three iron to twelve inches to secure victory.

I also won the German Masters by one shot from Payne Stewart and José María Olazábal. I was two behind Payne after three rounds but three early birdies gave me the lead, which I held to the end.

In 1989, I had some good finishes in the USA but it did not quite happen. I was second in the Federal Express St Jude Classic, three shots behind John Mahaffey. I was also third in the Heritage when Payne Stewart won.

During the practice day at Chepstow before the Epson Grand Prix, Peter Coleman told me that there were two people who wanted to see me so I came out to meet them. It was Andrew Wingfield Digby, director of Christians in Sport and Bruce Gillingham, a vicar from Birmingham. They introduced themselves and asked if I would be interested in having a Bible study on the European tour.

I replied that I had been at a prayer meeting earlier that week where, asked what my biggest prayer request was, I had replied, 'The establishment of a Bible study on the European tour.' Here was the answer to my prayer! I talked with Andrew and Bruce and we agreed to hold our first meeting at the PGA Championship at Wentworth in a week or two.

I was delighted with this development. I felt the need for a Bible study in Europe. I had benefited from attending the study in the USA and thought there must be a few people in Europe who would be interested. At that stage I did not feel knowledgable enough to lead it so I was looking for someone to take that role.

We held our first meeting at Wentworth. I put up some notices and the tour allowed us to use the boardroom. There was not a large number of players present but we had made a start.

We started initially at just a few tournaments, and it is still happening fourteen years on. Mark Pinney has replaced Bruce as the main leader. The sad thing is that it has not grown much in numbers. This partly reflects the fact that church attendance in Europe is much lower than in the USA. It is also the case that matters of faith are simply something that Europeans don't ever talk about. Americans are much more open in this way.

At the Bible study on the US tour, including players and their wives, caddies, etc. the attendance is anything from twenty to sixty. In Europe we are more likely to be between six and twelve. Sometimes we hold open meetings – often with my friend Hermann Gühring – where we deal with topics of more general interest.

I would love to see the numbers grow in Europe but we can only offer people the chance to attend; we cannot force them to come. When I think about all the strength and peace that I have gained from my relationship with God, it amazes me that so many of my fellow pros are able to get through life without apparently allowing God to be part of their life.

I know the joy and the security I get out of my relationship with God and I would love for others to have that too, but it's their choice. If they don't want it or they reject it, it's their fault. All you can do is to tell them about it and offer it and then it's up to them.

Chapter 10

The early 1990s

The years 1983–87 were a stretch in my life when I played very well, better than I had ever played before. Then came the despair of 1988 and the return of my putting problems. Having recovered from that in 1989, I then entered a period from 1991–95 when I won thirteen tournaments in Europe plus a second US Masters.

In 1990 I won the Cepsa Madrid Open with scores of 70, 67, 66 and 67. I entered the final day two ahead of Rodger Davis and finished one ahead. The final day surprise was Brett Ogle, who shot a 61 to finish two behind.

The Austrian Open took place at the Jack Nicklaus-designed Gut Altentann, Salzburg. I was in contention in the final round and reached the 498-yard eighteenth one behind Lanny Wadkins. When I pull-hooked my tee shot into the trees, my chances of winning seemed to have gone. There was a gap of about ten feet high and three feet wide through the trees. I went for it with a seven iron, and made it. I was 100 yards short, but put my wedge close to the pin and holed for an interesting birdie. Lanny, meanwhile, had gone through the green and taken five. We finished equal on 271 and seventeen under.

We set off on the play-off from the sixteenth. We halved the sixteenth and seventeenth and came again to the eighteenth. Lanny fluffed a chip, leaving me to get up and down from the bunker for victory.

* * *

An unexpected win that year was in the World Cup (team) at Grand Cypress, Florida. I had played for Germany in the World Cup five times previously, but without really being in the running. I felt that we were good enough to compete. However, most years when I played well I finished ten to fifteen shots ahead of my partner. To win it you need both players doing well.

It was an exceptional week and Torsten Giedeon played really well. He had just had to go to the tour qualifying school (trying to get his player's card for the European tour the next year) and failed. He was so down about it all that he didn't really want to talk about it. That we would do well that week was just about the most unlikely scenario you could visualise – he wasn't much fun to be around at the beginning of the week.

I tried to encourage him and, as the week went on, he started to believe in himself and to play well and we got into contention. We pulled each other along and in the end we became a team. I think we surprised a lot of people. We each shot 278 for fifth equal in the individual competition. The total of 556 was three ahead of England and Ireland. It was by far the biggest cheque Torsten had ever made in his life.

With two wins and five other top-three finishes I was fourth in the money list. It is a nice irony that after the despair of the late 1980s, I topped the European putting stats in 1990 with an average of 28.69 per round!

In 1991 I won four tournaments in three continents. The first was the Benson and Hedges International Open. The Benson and Hedges is one of those unfortunate tournaments that also seems to get the worst of the weather. For several years it was at St Mellion in Cornwall, in April or early May. Partly because of the weather they moved it inland. But when I won, in 1997 at the Oxfordshire, it was in some of the worst weather I have ever played. Seems like they couldn't win with the weather!

I had previously been second twice and also third, without winning. I felt at the end that I had finally broken the jinx. Remember that I had climbed a tree at Fulford in 1981 and done other crazy things to try to win this tournament. Now I had done it at last!

It was a strange tournament. I went up and down the leader-board like a yo-yo all week, with rounds of 73, 68, 75 and 70. I kept telling myself not to be discouraged. I was five behind with fourteen holes to play. A birdie on the eighth got me going and I came home in 32 with four more birdies. It all came down to the last few holes and I seemed to play a little better than the others, and also to hole the putts.

I finished on 286, two ahead of Vijay Singh. The conditions were so tough that I was the only player under par. Only twenty-eight players broke 300.

The other tournament that I won in Europe was the Mercedes German Masters, which was the week after the Ryder Cup and the infamous Kiawah Island putt. If it had not been the German Masters I think I would probably have taken the week off, but not only is the German Masters on home soil, it is also a tournament run by my brother and my company.

As I have written elsewhere, there is always extra pressure on me when I play in Germany because every journalist wants an interview. There is also the added burden of running the tournament and being available to the sponsors, VIPs, etc.

I really wanted the tournament to be a success and I really wanted to win it. Yet all everyone wanted to talk to me about was, 'What happened to you on that putt?' In the end I said I would talk about the putt on Wednesday and that would be the end of it. That was also when I told them that there had only been one perfect man and we crucified him; compared to that, missing a putt was really not so important.

I was not being difficult in not wanting to talk about the putt. The Bible gives us good advice when it says, 'Forget what is behind and work for what is ahead.' I don't live in the past, I live in the future. The putt at Kiawah Island missed; I am sorry that it missed but it happened and I cannot change it. There is no point in dwelling on it.

I reached the eighteenth green on the Sunday and was faced with a fifteen-foot putt to get into a play-off. It was hard to keep the events of the final green, seven days previously, out of my mind. I just prayed for help in keeping my concentration, lined up the putt and struck it – it went in! I beat Rodger Davis in the play-off.

I played in the Volvo PGA Championship at Wentworth, made the cut and finished fourth. The previous week in the Italian Open, I retired after one round with a shoulder injury. Technically I missed the cut.

Why am I mentioning that? Half the field misses the cut every week. While missing that cut did not seem significant at the time, in fact it was. In 1996 I played again in the Volvo PGA Championship, again at Wentworth and missed the cut. In between I had played sixty-seven tournaments on the European tour and made the cut in all of them. It was a sequence which, ironically, began and ended at Wentworth.

Looking back, I find that an almost unbelievable sequence. People ask me what is the secret of my consistency. It is hard to say. The previous record was fifty-six cuts made by Neil Coles. I had also had a run of fifty-four cuts made from 1983 to 1988. It is amazing to think that I twice played for four years without missing the cut, although I did come close on a number of occasions. There were a number of days when I did not feel comfortable with anything, but my short game pulled me through. I did drop out of one tournament (the European Masters in 1993) with injury but that was deemed not to count as a missed cut.

* * *

I won the 1991 Hong Kong Open. I finished with a 63. I was aware that Nick Faldo held the record at 62, and I was thinking about the record, but decided that it was better to concentrate on winning the tournament. You cannot buy anything with a course record!

I also won the Sun City Million Dollar Classic again – the richest prize in golf. I really like Sun City. Every shot is a challenge. You have to think your way around the course and that is something that suits me. I had an eight-shot lead going into the final round, and wondered if I should try to play safe. However, on many of the holes the pin positions were set to give you no safe shot. I decided to go for them. My 272 and sixteen under was at that time the championship record. It was also 34 better than my worst performance at Sun City when suffering the putting afflictions.

Everything went right that week, including my second shot to the 528-yard second hole. I decided to go for the green over water and I didn't catch it perfectly. However, it cleared the water, hit a rock and bounced forward to safety. On another day I would have bounced back and into the water.

It was at Sun City where I had one of the better introductions. Jim Furyk's swing has been described as an octopus trying to get out of a telephone box, but he is a very successful player. Dale Hayes introduced us by saying that, with Jim Furyk's backswing and Bernhard Langer's follow-through, you could tie a few knots! He was referring, of course, to the way I sometimes do the helicopter loop at the top of the follow-through.

I finished the year three days before Christmas, coming second to Fred Couples in the inaugural Johnnie Walker World Championship, which took my year's tournament earnings past $2 million.

* * *

In 1992 I won the Heineken Dutch Open in a play-off. With rounds of 68, 68 and 69, I entered the last round one ahead of Mike McLean. We both shot 72 so I stayed one ahead. Gordon Brand Jnr started the final round five behind me but, with a round of 67, he made up the deficit. Mike was unfortunate as he 'finished' one ahead of me, only to be told that he had been awarded a two-shot penalty for moving or bending the brambles, when his ball landed among them at the eleventh. We halved the first extra hole but, on the second, Gordon's approach to the green hit the grandstand. I won it with a par.

I won the Honda Open at Gut Kaden, near Hamburg, with rounds of 69, 65, 70 and 69, beating Darren Clarke by three. That was the same week as the World Matchplay, but I opted to compete in Germany. Good decision!

I finished first equal in the BMW International Open with Paul Azinger, Anders Forsbrand, Glen Day and Mark James. That was the oddest play-off I have ever been involved in, as five players drove off together. Paul Azinger hit the worst drive of the five, put it on the green, holed the putt and took the money. Another example of not how but how many!

1993 was dominated by my second US Masters win, but I also won the Volvo PGA Championship and the Volvo German Open. In the PGA my scores were 70, 69, 67 and 68. I was three shots off the lead at halfway, but ended up winning by six.

On the tenth hole on the first round, I shanked a shot. It went forty yards right. That was a bit of a shock; I hadn't shanked a ball for four years. I started the final round three shots ahead and managed to eagle the twelfth for the second day running, with a one iron from 211 yards to one foot, and to follow that with a birdie on the thirteenth. It was fun to play the final few holes with a big lead, knowing that all I had to do was avoid silly mistakes.

I duffed my tee shot on the fourteenth – I told the press I had a bad lie! It isn't often that you win a tournament with a shank and a duff but then I like to be different. Don't forget I have also won a tournament with two air-shots!

The Sunday was a busy day for me as we had an early morning Christian service on the eighteenth green, organised by Christians in Sport, with Bruce Gillingham speaking. Gavin Levenson and I also took part. A number of spectators joined in the service while many more were aware of it as it was broadcast around the course on the PA system.

In the Volvo German Open I led from day one and with scores of 65, 68, 70 and 66, I won by five strokes from Peter Baker. I said afterwards that if I putted like I did in that tournament for the rest of my life, I would be satisfied.

I also played in the World Cup at Lake Nona, Florida, and won the individual first prize by three shots. My partner was Sven Strüver and we came eighth in the team competition, with Davis Love and Fred Couples winning on home soil.

Having won the Masters and the European PGA, I was confident of a good run in the US Open, but picked up a neck injury at the wrong time. I could not prepare for the tournament the way I wanted to and missed the cut.

I had a good Open Championship at Sandwich in 1993. That was a busy week all round. I signed a new contract with Wilson and received from them a trophy to commemorate my two Masters wins with Wilson clubs. On the Tuesday night I spoke at a Christians in Sport golf clinic and dinner at Dover Castle. During the clinic I was stressing the importance of a good stance. I said that when I play in pro-ams I can usually tell how well one of the amateurs will play just by looking at their stance.

Someone in the crowd challenged me to give a demonstration and a number of people showed me their set-up. I did pretty well in assessing them on the whole. I have to watch what I say on these occasions as it seems to find its way into the press. On another occasion I said that I thought I could save a few shots every round if I was allowed to have sixteen clubs instead of fourteen. My thinking was that with two extra wedges you would always have the right club for your pitch shot. Sure enough, the *Daily Telegraph* ran the story next day that I was advocating a change to the rules of golf!

At the press conference before that Open Championship I had to deal with an unusual story. It had been reported in some newspapers that I was giving up golf to become a Christian missionary. I have no idea where the story came from, but I was happy to assure them that I planned to be winning tournaments for another ten to fifteen years.

I caused some members of the golfing press to lose their money that week. On the Saturday I was in the last group with Nick Faldo. With slowcoaches Langer and Faldo together and no one behind them, the scribes and photographers apparently were taking bets on the length of the round. Predictions were, I'm told, as high as four hours forty minutes for the two-ball. It hurts me to think of them losing their money – but we were round in three hours forty-eight!

I had an unusually inconsistent performance in the Alfred Dunhill Open with scores of 72, 64, 72 and 65. If you manage to shoot 64 you should give yourself a good chance of winning but in the end I finished three behind winner, Darren Clarke.

I won the Canon Champions Shoot-out in 1993. These events are always great fun, played in a skins format with a lot of banter between the players. My victory secured a cheque for £12,000 for the Charing Cross Hospital in London.

In the USA I was second to Nick Price in the Players' Championship at Sawgrass. He opened with a 64 and I never managed to close the gap.

In 1994 I won the Murphy's Irish Open. It was quite a

battle. After three rounds I was four behind Robert Allenby. In the final round I was out in 31 with five birdies. I also birdied the sixteenth to finish with a 67 and one ahead of Allenby and John Daly.

I knew John Daly – who shot a final round 65 – was on a charge, but I came out of the blocks pretty fast myself. I could have made the victory easier for myself – in the third round I hit sixteen greens but only made two birdies.

I have always loved the game of golf, from the moment I discovered it as an eight-year-old caddie. I have also always loved competition. Pitting my ability against another competitor has always got my adrenaline flowing. Being in a situation where I need to make up four shots in the final round to win is one I thrive on.

The Volvo Masters at Valderrama included probably my best-ever round so far. Valderrama is a course where you have to use your brains. You have to position the ball and manoeuvre it. There are a few holes where three wood or one iron off the tee is a sensible option. The fairways are narrow, so hitting it straight off the tee is vital.

On some holes hitting the green is an achievement but even then, if you are above the hole, you can have a very difficult putt on very fast greens. It has a difficult finish. The seventeenth is a hole where it is possible to make anything from an eagle to an eight. I would not have designed the hole like that. I think it would be much better if they put some rough between the green and the water, or I would have made the green deeper. The eighteenth is a tough finishing hole where a good drive goes over the first oak tree and stops before the second.

In the second round I shot 62. In the scorer's tent I wasn't so much counting my score as checking that I had played all eighteen holes! The 62 was all the more remarkable as I did not break 70 in any of the other rounds. I was two behind Seve going into the final round and did not take the lead until the seventeenth, finally beating Vijay Singh and Seve by one. It is always good to beat Seve in Spain.

There was a bit of controversy towards the finish, when Seve called for a ruling. His ball came to rest at the foot of a tree to the right of the fairway. Referee John Paramor, who had fined Seve for slow play the previous day, ruled that there were no grounds for relief. Seve failed to make par and lost by one.

Seve and I have become pretty good friends over the years and are getting closer and closer. We are the same age, both married with kids and we've both gone through highs and lows, so there are a lot of things in common even though we are two very different people. We have had dinner a few times, play practice rounds together and we have often met up in the physio unit. At times we've probably seemed to be the two main clients there.

I may have won in Spain but could not win in Germany. I opened up pretty well with rounds of 69, 68 and 65 in the German Open at Düsseldorf, but still found myself three behind Colin Montgomerie. I had three birdies in the first six holes but could only find one more in the next twelve. I finished with a 68 and one behind Colin.

In 1995 I had three wins in Europe: the Volvo PGA Championship, the Deutsche Bank Open-TPC of Europe and the Smurfit European Open. I won the Volvo PGA Championship at Wentworth by one shot from Michael Campbell and Per-Ulrik Johansson. This was my first win of that year, and the seventeenth consecutive year that I had slipped into the winners' circle. The PGA Championship is a special event for me. It is the players' own event, one of the biggest tournaments in the year. It is always a very competitive tournament and a hard one to win.

After three rounds I was equal with Mark Mouland and one ahead of Per-Ulrik Johansson. Mark fell away and I stayed one ahead of Per-Ulrik as we both shot 71s. Michael Campbell's 67 gave me a few anxious moments. I was out in par – one birdie and one bogey cancelling each other – but dropped a shot at the thirteenth. I missed the green with a nine iron and then fluffed a chip. Fortunately I managed to hit a seven iron to four feet at the par-three fourteenth to keep it going.

The European Open at the K Club near Dublin is a good example of how things can change and how, as the Bible puts it, we should persevere to the end. I started badly, with a 74, and was in danger of missing the cut. A 70 saw me safely around for the weekend. After a 68 in the third round, I was only three short of the lead. I played steadily in the final round but was always struggling to catch the leader. The final hole is 518 yards and, with the help of the wind, I was on it in two. When I holed a seventy-foot eagle putt for a 70 in the fourth round, I was joint leader with Barry Lane.

When that putt went in I jumped in the air and got some stick from the press. Come on! If you can't get excited about holing a seventy-foot putt on the seventy-second hole to tie the lead, what can you get excited about? Barry Lane was two holes behind me and his putt to win rimmed the hole and stayed up.

I won the play-off at the second hole. We played the eighteenth and both birdied it. On the tenth Barry was bunkered with his second, but all but holed the bunker shot. I holed the birdie putt from twenty-two feet to win. It is always great to win a play-off, but you feel for the loser. Barry had led most of the tournament and had seemed to have it won until I got the eagle.

I won the Deutsche Bank Open with four rounds in the 60s. A 67 in the first round gave me the lead and I never lost it. I just played pretty well all week and putted well. After I had birdied six of the first twelve holes of the tournament, one of the caddies remarked, 'Give him the money now and we can all go home!' A nice idea, but they made me play another three days. There is a saying in the game, 'Beware of the sick golfer', and I was fighting off 'flu all week. I was feeling awful but playing well!

I had a real chance to win the American Players' Championship in 1995. After three rounds I was tied for the lead with Corey Pavin, one ahead of Lee Janzen. Both Corey and I dropped shots early on and Lee birdied the second to take the lead. A double bogey at the fourteenth really ended my chance and put Lee three ahead. Although I birdied the fifteenth and eighteenth, it was not enough. Lee won by a shot.

The mid-1990s were a period of success to rival my mid-1980s. But just to show me that you can take nothing for granted in this game, 1996 was just around the corner.

Chapter 11

A memorable Easter Sunday

I had won the US Masters in 1985. I suppose I expected it to be easy to win more majors. I had come close to adding other major titles, notably the Open Championship, on two or three occasions. I had succumbed to the yips in 1988 and had beaten them again. By the early 1990s I was more determined than ever to win another major.

My performances in the Masters had been solid. I had made the cut every year since 1984 and had had three top-ten finishes. My best chance to win had been in 1987, when I had been one off the lead with nine holes to play but had then dropped shots in four of six holes to finish on 40 for the back nine. That was the year Larry Mize beat Greg Norman and Seve in the play-off by holing a chip from thirty yards.

In 1993 I made a solid start, playing well in the opening two rounds for 68 and 70. So, at the halfway stage, I was tied with Don Forsman. I had an excellent round of 69 on the Saturday in windy conditions and that gave me a four-shot lead going into the final round. I had never been in that position in a major before.

Four shots seems a lot but in a round at Augusta, anything is possible – especially when you are playing against the best players in the world. I couldn't help remembering that in 1985, Curtis Strange was four shots ahead of me with nine to play. If I could make up four shots on nine holes, I could also lose four shots. The tournament was far from over and I could not afford to be complacent. There is no guarantee in golf.

1996 was still in the future, but the way Greg Norman started with a six-shot lead and finished up losing by four to Nick Faldo confirms what can happen in the Masters.

I knew that I had the best chance to win but I was still a little nervous. I played pretty solid on the first nine holes, which I always find harder than the back nine with fewer birdie opportunities. I was level at the turn, but the problem was that everyone else was playing better. My four-shot lead had slipped to one by the eleventh. Chip Beck, who was my playing partner, and Dan Forsman, who was a hole ahead, were my two closest rivals. As Chip had won the par-three competition, tradition was against him winning the tournament – but as I've mentioned, I don't believe in superstitions like that!

The eleventh green is just by the twelfth tee – the par-three. I was on the edge of the green, waiting for Forsman to tee off before I played. He put his tee shot in the water, and he put his next shot in the water as well. I knew he was then out of contention. I all but holed my chip and made par.

That meant that it was effectively down to Chip Beck and me. As we were playing together, it was like matchplay. The thirteenth was a big hole. In 1993 it was 465 yards but the green is protected by water. I outdrove Chip, taking a tight line down the left. He put his second on the green to set up an eagle opportunity. I had to go for the green with a three iron off a sidehill lie and over water. I made it! He made birdie but I holed the eagle putt to increase my lead to two shots. It was a big putt with about three inches of break.

That shows how tight it is and how small the margins are between success and failure.

When Chip's ball was already on the green and I was hitting my second, I could have missed the green, and gone in the water or one of the many bunkers, and only par or even bogey or double. Instead I made eagle and gained a shot.

It is a good example of how Augusta has changed over the years. In 1993 the thirteenth was 465 yards. Now it is 510 yards. Again the fourteenth, which that year was 405 yards is now 440 yards. On the fourteenth we were both on the green in two and made par. I all but holed the birdie putt.

On the 500-yard fifteenth, another hole with water, I decided to lay up with my second shot. There was no reason for me to take a risk with the water as I needed only to match Chip in the closing holes. After I played he seemed to take an age to decide what to do. Peter and I said to each other, 'Surely he has got to go for it if he's going to try to win the tournament?' But he decided to lay up. My pitch was close to the flag but he was through the back. I holed the birdie putt but Chip had to settle for a par. So it was pretty much over, with a three-shot lead and three holes to play.

People ask me, on a hole like the fifteenth at Augusta, how I decide whether or not to go for the green in two. That is a good example. The first factor is that you must be close enough and have a good enough lie to be able to reach the green. The second factor is the state of the game. If I had been in Chip's position, I would almost certainly have gone for the green to try to make eagle and to put me under pressure. By laying up he made it easier for me.

The sixteenth is the par-three with water all down the left. I played safe and landed in the middle of the green. It left me with a long downhill putt with a lot of swing. I hit it about three feet past and holed for par.

It was such a nice feeling, playing the last two holes with the cushion of a five-stroke lead, not having to worry about how to play those holes. I knew that if I kept the ball in play, I would win.

The seventeenth is 400 yards. My drive was good but I hit a poor approach shot, missing the green on the right. However, I saved par with a chip and a putt. On the eighteenth, I hit my second into a greenside bunker. I played a safe bunker shot and took two putts. The round started and ended with bogey but in between I had done enough to secure the win.

I was fairly calm all week. I had the confidence to believe that I would play well and possibly win. I was aware of friends praying for me. Two people rang me to say that while they were praying for me they had had a sense that I was going to win. My mother had had the same feeling. All these people saying that gave me real confidence that it could happen.

The 1993 Masters finished on Easter Sunday. As usual I was taken into the Butler Cabin for the live TV interview. The first question I was asked was how the first Masters win compared with the second. I answered, 'It's a great honour to win the greatest tournament in the world, and especially on Easter Sunday, the day my Lord was resurrected.'

In saying those words, which went round the world on live television, I hope I was able to make up for my shortcomings in 1985 by saying something more positive. Having the opportunity of sharing with the world my faith in Jesus Christ was, for me, a unique situation.

People have asked me which Masters victory gave me the most pleasure. I really cannot answer that – they were both special in their own way. The earlier one was my first major and my first win in the USA. Not a lot of people expected me to win. The second time, I had become a believer and I won on Easter Sunday, which was a very special day for me.

Some people may not understand that, but it was very meaningful for me as a believer to have won on the day that we celebrate that Jesus Christ was raised from the dead. You see, I strongly believe that the resurrection of Jesus actually happened. There were about 500 eye-witnesses who saw him alive again. I believe that it takes more faith not to believe in Jesus Christ than to believe in him. Don't take my word for it – check it yourself.

Chapter 12

Developments in the game

I am including this chapter in the book for those who are particularly interested in some of the technical aspects of golf. I started playing golf when I was eight, with about four shared clubs in the caddie shack. I have seen a few changes in golf equipment in the next thirty-something years.

When I was about thirteen I had saved enough money from caddying to buy my first set of golf clubs. They were Kroydons. I remember how exciting it was to have wedges – having not used anything more lofted than a seven before – and all the right clubs, which previously I did not have. I really loved those golf clubs and was so proud of them.

My first contract, when I became a professional, was with Spalding. Then I played with Ben Hogan clubs for eight years. I used Wilson clubs for twelve years. I was sorry to leave Wilson – it was their decision, not mine. They had just launched the fat shaft and wanted to put all their marketing effort into that. I tried it but did not like it. They said that unless I used the fat shaft, I had no future with Wilson. As I did not want to play with that shaft I had no choice but to find new clubs.

Then I played Ping for one year. As I said, that change was thrust upon me and I did not want to make the mistake I had seen other players make – of changing clubs for a good contract, only to find that they could not play with the equipment. So I practised hard for two months with the Ping clubs. After two months I felt I was playing at about 90 to 95 per cent with the new clubs and decided I could use them.

It was a big change but I felt that the last 5 to 10 per cent would come gradually. However, I was never totally convinced and comfortable with the clubs, though I cannot say for certain that the clubs were the problem. Perhaps I was struggling a bit with my swing. I was not controlling shots as well as I used to; I was hitting one shot further, another shot not quite as far as I expected or to one side or other, but not quite where I wanted to.

The problem is that at the level at which I play, just one shot per round can make the difference between winning and being fifth. When you hit the ball as far as professionals do, being off-line by just 1 per cent sends the ball a long way from the target. That 1 or 2 per cent can make the difference and I felt that I was losing at least 5 per cent. It just didn't work out.

I was working hard with Ping to develop a blade, which is more of a traditional club. They were trying to create a club that had the feel of a blade but retained the characteristic Ping look. It was a compromise and, to be frank, I was looking for a real blade as I had played blades all my life, but they did not want to go that far. We all worked hard and the new club we developed was very successful and popular but not quite what I was looking for. In the end we agreed that it was best simply to part company with no hard feelings on either side.

After Ping I went back to Ben Hogan clubs – blades, naturally. I have always liked the Hogan clubs and, of course, I had played with them for eight years earlier in my career. I had some very good years with them; they are very much the type of club I grew up playing. They look very traditional. However, it had been fifteen years since I had used Hogan clubs. As I was free to choose, I decided to give them another try.

It's a good partnership. I had a positive attitude towards the clubs and Hogan wanted to sign me. I flew out to meet them, tried the clubs and felt comfortable from the start. I was sure I could play well with them. Hogan had three or four sets they thought could be suitable for me.

There have been major changes in club technology during my career. I started with steel shafts and wooden heads. Now they are all graphite shafts and titanium heads. Because they are lighter, the shaft has become longer. This generates more clubhead speed. As I have got older I have lost some strength, but the development in clubs means that I am hitting the ball as far – if not further – than ever. The problem is that everyone else is also hitting it further!

In my bag I have a driver and three wood and a putter. As far as irons go, I always have three to nine plus sand, pitch and lob wedge. My fourteenth club is a choice between a five wood and a two iron. I hit the five wood and the two iron the same distance. The five wood goes higher than the two iron. So the decision is made according to the design of the course and the weather conditions.

As you will have gathered, I like blades. Apart from the year when I played Pings, I have always used blades. I like the feel and the look. I like V grooves – the only disadvantage is getting flyers out of the rough, which are difficult to control. But it is what I am used to and what I am comfortable with. My wedges have U grooves.

When I am getting a new set of clubs, I tell the manufacturers a few things I like. For example, I like the leading edge of a club to be rounded off. I don't want it sharp. I like the bottom of the club rounded and not dead straight. I think it goes through the ground a little more easily. The changes are so slight that most people wouldn't notice when they look at the clubs but I like the feel of clubs with these adjustments.

Then I tell them how much offset I want in the clubs. The angles of my irons are standard. At 1.73 metres in height, I am not one of the bigger players so I have my clubs made a bit flatter than the more upright club a taller person would use.

Based on that information, the manufacturers will make me up a set of clubs. They would certainly be usable but there will still be a few adjustments I would want. For example, I might want to put a little more weight on the long irons, to get the ball more up in the air.

I do my distances in metres. The various clubs go like this:

Pitching wedge	110 metres	
Seven iron	150 metres	
Three iron	190 metres	
Three wood	210 metres	(carry)
Driver	230 metres	(carry)

With all clubs, of course you can hit it straight or try to work it. Generally speaking, a fade will go three to five metres less, a slice ten metres less, a draw three to five metres further and a hook ten metres further.

As part of the contract with Spalding, I also changed to the Strata ball. I did a lot of testing before I signed up to use it and it's a great ball. Yet, having played the Titleist ball for many years, it was quite a big change for me. (Spalding makes Strata and owns Hogan.)

I had played a wound ball all my career, but I am now convinced that multi-layer construction is the future. Multi-layer balls are longer off the driver and a little longer off the long irons but spin like a wound ball around the greens. The durability of a solid-core ball is much better.

Balata is now history. The technology has come so far that they can now make the two- or three-piece ball from this material, with similar spin. It feels a little harder and goes further. The new ball has all the best features of the old balata but also added distance. With a balata, if you caught the ball a bit thin, you put a mark on it. These new balls last a lot longer. When I signed to play Strata it was not just a case of being given one ball – they had five or six different types for me to choose from.

As clubs and balls have developed, everyone is hitting the ball further. That has led to great debates in the golf press as to whether some equipment should be banned in order to restrict the distance players can hit. Some holes, where fifteen years ago players would have needed two woods to hit the green, are now reachable for Tiger, Davis Love and the like, with a driver and a short iron.

I have listened to all the arguments and these are my opinions. Perhaps there is a case for stopping the constant development of clubs and balls that produce greater distance, but I think it is hard to go backwards and try to undo the progress of the last few years. I don't think you can reverse the process by insisting on a ball that will go 30 per cent less far than at present. Again, if you try to legislate for the speed the ball can come off the club head, how on earth do you police it? It just isn't practical.

There are also implications for the golf industry. Golf manufacturers need to sell their products and grow. Much of the golf trade is based on the search for products that are better and will make you play better. If you ban new equipment you take away the fun for the player and damage your own industry.

One of the fascinations of golf is to hit the ball a long way. If you introduce a ball that does not go as far, you take away the great thrill for golfers at all levels. John Daly has always had one of the biggest followings on the tour – because people like seeing him hit the ball a long way. If he hit the ball fifty yards less I don't think he would have half the following he has.

One of the problems I do see with the developments in the equipment – clubs and balls – is that an average player with good equipment can play shots which, a few years ago, only a great player could do. That means that the gap between the great players and the average players is being narrowed –

because of the equipment. The really good players who, in the past, could manufacture great shots with the limited equipment, are now seeing their advantage eroded. An average player with modern clubs can produce similar shots these days. Without a doubt the progress in equipment has brought everyone closer together.

When I decided to play the Strata ball, they offered me six different balls to find the one that suited my game best. When I started out as a tournament pro there were perhaps six decent balls in total. Now each manufacturer has six different balls.

Some people ask if it would be fairer for all players in a tournament to use the same ball – like in a tennis tournament. That would make a big difference – especially if it was a different ball each week. It is an interesting concept. Would Tiger still be number one? I think so. But would he be further ahead than he is now, or less? Who knows? It would certainly reward skill, as every player would just have to use that ball and make the best of it. The players would have to accommodate the ball, rather than everyone having a ball that accommodates their flight and launch pattern.

Playing a different ball every week would be very difficult, as they would all go different distances, with different trajectories. Changing every week would be very confusing. If it was decided to go that way, you would have to pick a ball and have everyone play with it for the year. Players would want a month or two to practise in different conditions and get used to it.

Another problem with that idea is that it would kill the ball market. At present a large percentage of the public buys a particular ball because their favourite player uses it. The retail golf market is driven by the professionals. So it would hit the golf industry hard, and it would hurt the players too as we would no longer get ball contracts.

I suppose much of this is driven by a desire to protect the golf course, to stop someone shooting a 55. That is a difficult issue. There are some great old courses, which have been around for perhaps a hundred years. Sadly, I think it is impossible to protect them. They are too short. You need to increase the length by moving the tees back, but some of them have no room to do that. Augusta is an old course with a great tradition, but they keep changing it, lengthening it so that it represents the same challenge to the players today as it did ten or fifteen years ago.

They recently added 300 yards to the course to take it to 7,270 yards. They now have four par-four holes that are over 460 yards. The eighteenth is a good example. Everyone remembers Sandy Lyle driving into the bunker in the final round the year he won. When Tiger won he carried that bunker by a mile, leaving himself just a wedge of seventy-five yards. Now they have added sixty yards to the hole, bringing that bunker back into play for most people.

I think the only solution is to make courses longer. The golf courses I am designing now are much longer than the ones I was designing fifteen years ago. I used to position bunkers 230–255 yards from the back tee. Now it is 255–280, or even 300 yards, because the guys are carrying it so much further. Good course design will have a series of tees, so that you bring the bunkers into play for everyone – from the pro, who is driving 280 yards, to the medium handicapper who is hitting it 200 yards.

Some courses are designed with a lot of holes where it is a risky to use the driver off the tee. That is one solution. But it is not very exciting for the player or the spectator if players are hitting a lot of irons from the tee. I am all for a few holes with narrow fairways and well-protected small greens, but you can't build a whole course like that.

To sum up, there is no doubt that the development in equipment has caused some problems, but I feel that many of the solutions proposed would cause more problems than they would solve.

Chapter 13

Success with a long handle

1996 was the year that the yips came back again. It was a hard year. Not only was I putting badly, but I also had problems with my swing for part of that year. After putting successfully for several years with the split cross-handed grip, my putting deteriorated in 1996. That is when I started using the long handle. I won only once that year, the Alfred Dunhill Masters in Hong Kong. It was the first time since 1979 that I had not won a tournament in Europe. My thirty-ninth place in the Volvo Ranking (European money list) was also my worst place since 1979.

I played fifteen tournaments in Europe and the French was my only top-ten finish. Having not missed a cut in Europe for five years, I missed three in 1996. The first missed cut was at the PGA Championship. That was disappointing as I was the defending champion. The week had started well with Adidas presenting me with a pair of golden golf shoes to celebrate the fact that I had walked 5,000 miles around golf courses in Adidas shoes.

The problem was as much with the golf as the putting. My opening round of 73 contained only 26 putts. In the second round I shot 74 – it was just a scrappy round. I bogeyed the first three holes. It contained bad shots as much as bad putts. Even then I had a chance to make the cut as I was just one over with four to play. I missed the green at the fifteenth,

114

three-putted the seventeenth and missed birdie chances on the sixteenth and eighteenth.

In one sense it was just what Jimmy Connors used to call 'a bad day at the office'. That the run of cuts would end some time was inevitable. As it was only my third tournament in Europe that year, I just saw it as a bad week. As the year progressed I came to see it as a week typical of my year.

I injured my shoulder and seemed to go on a downward spiral. I was disqualified in the US Open when I signed for the wrong score – although, as I would have missed the cut anyhow, it made no difference. I also had to retire through injury after the first round of the Open Championship.

I used the long-handled (forty-eight-inch) putter for the first time in a tournament at the Lancôme in Paris. It felt a bit awkward but it went well. I completed the first nine holes in 30 – five under – and the round in 67. I didn't quite manage to keep that going but I finished fifteenth and was delighted with that as a first attempt with the new putter.

Some of the press described it as a last resort. I didn't see it that way. I had conquered my putting problems twice before through hard work and a change of technique. For me the use of the long putter was just another technical change. With God in my life I had the strength and determination to do what I thought was the right thing to solve the problem I had.

The only encouragement of the year came in the Alfred Dunhill Masters in Hong Kong. I was three behind after three rounds. Having got into the lead, I nearly threw it away on the par-three fifteenth hole. While Kang Wook Soon made birdie, I made five. My tee shot was too strong and took a hard bounce through the green. Then I fluffed a chip, chipped on and took two putts.

I managed to stay positive and, as we walked to the sixteenth tee, I told Peter that I could still win. Peter was a bit tired that day as he had stayed up half the night to watch his beloved

Chelsea beat Manchester United. He told me that if Chelsea could win at Old Trafford, I should be able to win in Hong Kong.

There had been a three-stroke swing at the fifteenth, but to show how quickly things can change, there was a two-stroke swing in the opposite direction at the sixteenth, when I holed from fifteen feet for birdie and Kang took five. I regained and held the lead, shooting a round of 65 to win by two.

This was my first win for thirteen months. It was the fourth tournament in which I had used the long putter and I was encouraged to be competitive with it so soon. Thirteen months without a win was a long time and it was especially satisfying to prove that I could win with the long putter. The greens were not the easiest, but I don't think I could have putted much better. I said at the time that I don't care what it looks like – in golf you don't get paid for what it looks like but for results.

Playing with Alexander Cejka in the World Cup in South Africa, I came third in the individual and we were fourth in the team competition. With Ernie Els and Wayne Westner first and second in the individual competition, it was a comfortable win for the home team.

As I prepared for 1997, when I would turn forty, I still believed that my best years were not all behind me. I felt as hungry for victory as ever.

After the stutter the previous year, 1997 proved to be an excellent year with four wins in Europe. I finished second in the order of merit, behind Colin Montgomerie. I also won the Argentinian Masters. I started with a seventh at the Johnnie Walker Classic and was fourth in the Dubai Desert Classic. Then in May the season really took off.

I won the Comte of Florence Italian Open at Bresca. I had thought all week that José María Olazábal was the man to beat and I started the final round three shots behind him. I thought I would need to shoot 65 or 66 to win. I started with a birdie and added three more to be out in 32. I knew I had to stay aggressive on the back nine. I dropped a shot on the tenth but birdied the eleventh.

On the short seventeenth, the pin was close to the water; I went for it and finished on a down-slope in the bunker. I managed to get it out to twelve feet and holed the putt for par. On the eighteenth I took the driver rather than the safer one iron. I ended up in the rough – only just – and was able to make the green. When I holed for birdie, it was the first time I had been ahead all week. My four birdies in the last five holes took me to eight under, a round of 64 and a win by one shot. It was great to win again after the barren year in 1996.

It was also great to start the year so well. A few months previously I had been really struggling, both with my health and my game, especially the putting. I suffered a shoulder injury and my forearms were tense and tight. I had muscle spasms and this definitely did not help my putting, as you can only putt well if you are relaxed and loose. Over the winter I worked hard on my health and fitness and felt a lot better in 1997. The long putter had also contributed to my confidence on the greens.

The following week I won again, this time in England – the Benson and Hedges International Open at the Oxfordshire by two shots from Ian Woosnam. I started the final round one ahead of Ian and my playing partner, Lee Westwood. The weather was not kind that week – wind and rain as well as being very cold. In fact the final day's play was interrupted by the weather when I still had six holes to play. Seve commented that in England you should not play golf before June.

My game plan in the final round was to take the birdies if they came along but generally make pars. Don't make bogey or double. That meant that the others had to take the risks if they were going to get to me – and the conditions were not easy.

The seventeenth hole at the Oxfordshire is an interesting one. It is 585 yards with a lake. The 'correct' way to play it is to keep the lake on your left, following the fairway as it curves round the lake, taking three shots to reach the green. If your drive is OK you have the option of going for the green in two but anything short is in the water. There is a third option of going left of the lake. This is the hole where some years ago Padraig Harrington put his second in the water, could not believe that he had not carried the water, repeated the shot twice and put those in the water too – finishing with a thirteen on the hole!

The seventeenth is a good example of how I make course management decisions. The seventeenth tee is a fifty-yard walk back from the sixteenth green. Usually the players go and the caddies walk up the fairway. I might take three clubs to the tee – driver, three wood and two iron.

You do not know exactly where the tee will be. Sometimes they move the tee right back. If I cannot reach the green in two, either because the wind is against me or because the tee is too far back, there is no point in hitting driver and bringing the water into play. By hitting the iron or three wood you take the water out of play. Even if you hit a bad shot left, it will still be short of the water and playable. Of course you have a longer second shot but as you cannot reach the green in two, that is not a problem. But if I think I can reach the green in two, I might take a chance with the water, hit driver and leave myself as short a second shot as possible.

In the final round that year I was in the lead at the time. I think Lee was one behind me. He took driver and went for the green in two, but didn't quite make it. His ball went in the water and he took six. I laid up to the left of the lake with my second, hit a good wedge and holed the putt for four. Lee had hit a good tee shot and, I guess, was borderline whether he could reach the green or not.

Also as he was one shot behind he had to take a chance and

have a go for the green. I hit three good shots the safe way and made a putt for birdie. Of course, sometimes it works the other way – he could have hit a good shot and made eagle and I could have missed the putt and just made par. But that is golf – you never know until it's over.

My only mistake in Sunday's round was a dropped shot at the short second. There was a break of an hour and forty minutes after I had played twelve holes, because of hail. It was a good break for me. When we resumed, the wind had died down and conditions were much easier. I had spent the break stretching and keeping loose in the locker room.

With two wins on the roll, I would have expected better than I got from the next few tournaments. I followed a 67 at the PGA with rounds of 75 and 76, missed the cut at the Deutsche Bank Open, the Irish Open and the Loch Lomond World Invitational.

I arrived in Prague for the Chemapol Trophy Czech Open, fresh from a family holiday in Portugal. The Karlstein Golf Club is situated on a hilltop, overlooked by a fourteenth-century fortress. My opening round of 70 included a triple bogey seven at the fifth. With scoring very low, it left me in fifty-fifth place. A second-round 67 left me thirtieth and still six behind. A third-round 64 took me to fifth but still four behind. I still needed something special to win and I found it in a 63 (against par 71) to win by four. I was very pleased with the sharpness of my short game despite the two-week lay-off.

On the seventeenth I had had another of those course management decisions to make. The hole is 514 yards and I had hit a good drive. The green was within range but there was a valley of thick undergrowth between me and the green. I took the three wood, found the green and got the birdie.

The press made a bit of my winning the Czech Open because of my father. But he isn't really Czech. He was living in the German part of what later became Czechoslovakia. I have sometimes read that he is Czech-born but I don't think that is true. One Czech who was in the field that week was Ivan Lendl. Unfortunately he missed the cut.

At the BMW International Open in Munich, they presented me with a golden club to mark fifty tournament victories. It was the only golden club I had that week as I finished six behind Robert Karlsson. I was in a good position in the Lancôme until a final round 75 ended my chances.

My fourth European tour victory was in the Linde German Masters in Berlin, the week after the Ryder Cup. I wasn't really aware of it until someone pointed it out to me, but it was the third time I had won the week after Ryder Cup – in 1991 in the German Masters and in 1995 in the Smurfit European Open. I am simply a player who forgets the past and focuses on the future.

I led from the front but really set up the victory with a 60 on the Saturday, with an eagle and eleven birdies. Incredibly, it could have been a 58. I had a three-putt from twenty feet and a three-footer, which lipped out. If I had only taken two putts and holed my three-footer, which I normally would, I would have made 58. But there are a lot of 'shoulds' and 'woulds' in golf. To shoot a round like this you basically need to play almost flawless golf and then hole the putts. In the 60 I had one chip in for eagle. I hit good shots, set up birdie chances and holed the putts – apart from those two occasions. My playing partner, José María Olazábal, said I played like ET!

I was delighted. I holed a lot of putts. I had never shot twelve under in a competition before. You never know when this sort of thing is going to happen and it felt especially good that in happened in Germany.

Whether it is my best ever round is hard to answer. It is certainly the lowest score and the only time I was twelve under, but the 62s at Valderrama and El Saler were on tougher courses.

My second round 69 included a double bogey six on the ninth hole (my eighteenth). My ball was in a sand-filled divot hole; I did not make a good contact with it and put it in the water.

I was amused when a golf magazine said that the purpose of the German Masters tournament was to provide employment for the Langer family, pointing out that I was playing in it and my brother Erwin was running the tournament. In addition my daughter Jackie and Erwin's daughter Maria were working on the scoreboards. My sister was running the shop and my wife and mother were looking after some of the players' children!

In 1998 I did not win at all. My best performances were second equal in the Peugeot Open de France, finishing two shots behind Sam Torrance. Sam opened with a 64 to my 71 – while I narrowed the gap to two shots, I never quite got close enough.

I was fourth in the BMW International Open behind Russell Claydon. In the Volvo Masters at Montecastillo, I holed in one with a seven iron at the 172-yard fourteenth in a third round of 67, but still finished five behind winner, Darren Clarke.

In 1999 again I did not win but I did come close, with two second-place finishes. In January I finished second to Jarrold Mosely in the Heineken Classic in Perth, Australia, by one shot.

In the Volvo Masters at Montecastillo I was second equal with Padraig Harrington and Retief Goosen, two behind Miguel Angel Jiménez. My final round of 66 contained five birdies, an eagle and a bogey, but I was never at any time in the lead. I could have done with repeating my hole in one at Montecastillo! The week was dedicated to the memory of Payne Stewart. I gave a short tribute in his memory at the end of the second round.

I was seeded twenty-fifth in the WGC Andersen Consulting Matchplay Tournament. I beat Brad Faxon four and two and

Vijay Singh two and one. In the last sixteen I lost by one hole to Jeff Maggert who was the eventual winner.

I threw away the Greg Norman Holden International tournament in Australia in the most unbelievable way. I shot 65 in the second round and found myself in the lead by one at the start of the final round. I came to the eighteenth needing a par for victory. I knocked the ball onto the green and marked the ball. I was preparing to putt, had my ball in my hand and picked up my marker – without putting the ball down. Usually I put the ball down in front of the marker. It's never happened before but it happened that day. Don't ask me why I did it – it just happened.

It is the dumbest thing I have ever done on the golf course. Perhaps I had heat stroke!

I had a putt, which I needed to hole to win the tournament. My routine in these situations is to put my coin down to mark it and give Peter the ball to clean. Then I ask Peter to put the ball down behind the coin – not in front or it would be in play. He puts it down behind the coin, so I can see the line when I'm looking from the other side of the hole.

So he puts the ball behind the coin and I look from both sides. Then when I'm ready to putt, I replace the ball and pick up the marker. But this time instead of placing the ball in front of the coin, I picked up the coin. As I had the coin in my fingers, and was just picking it up, it was still touching the ground at one side, I suddenly thought, 'What are you doing?' and put it down immediately. I thought I had better call the referee and I got two penalty shots. And the tournament was over for me. It was just a total blackout.

I finished with a triple bogey and I think it cost me A$112,500 but more importantly another victory.

I was involved in another odd incident in 1999, during the PGA Championship. I took a practice swing on the ninth hole. Someone who was watching on TV telephoned and said I had

The excitement is too much during the 1987 Ryder Cup.

Sandy Lyle gives me a helping hand.

With my friend Larry Nelson at the 1987 Ryder Cup after an epic match.

Good things come to those who wait! Sharing in the celebrations
of the first European Ryder Cup win for twenty-eight years,
with Sandy Lyle and Seve Ballesteros.

That putt! The shot that sealed the fate of the 1991 Ryder Cup.

Jackson Stephens is left holding the baby (Christina) at the 1993 US Masters!

Auditioning for the Ministry of Silly Walks during the 1993 US Masters.

Reading the lesson at the Sunday morning service during the
1993 Ryder Cup at the Belfry (Corey Pavin is behind me).

Using the broomhandle putter at the 1997 Dubai Desert Classic.

Arabian knight! At the 1997 Dubai Desert Classic.

Peter Coleman, caddie and friend.

My first hero –
Gary Player.

Payne Stewart. Sorely missed
this side of heaven.

broken a branch with my practice swing. The European tour chief referee, John Paramor, watched the video and then talked to me.

The issue was that had I been deemed to have improved the area of my intended swing, it would have been a two-shot penalty. However, he concluded that there was certainly a large degree of doubt whether the small branch that was broken off was actually in the area of the intended swing. There was no penalty and I finished in seventh place, eight shots behind Colin Montgomerie.

At Sun City I finished fifth. The way the course was set up, the length off the tee gave you a real advantage. The greens at Sun City are very hard and they can be very difficult to hold. It is obviously preferable to go in with a nine iron or wedge rather than a six or a seven iron, and if you are a long hitter that is certainly possible.

When I was playing with Davis Love in the second round, on the ninth I was hitting a three iron whereas he took a nine. Then on the tenth, I hit a good tee shot but still had to hit three wood whereas Davis only needed a six iron. That is a serious disadvantage I have to make up by being more precise with the long irons or playing a brilliant short game.

In 2000 I again failed to win but twice collected second place. I was second in the Dutch Open at Noordwijkse GC, four shots behind Stephen Leaney, and to Thomas Björn in the BMW International Open in Munich. I was seventeen under par but Thomas was twenty under. Every time I made birdie or eagle, he seemed to do the same.

A new competition for 2000 was the Severiano Ballesteros Trophy, a Ryder Cup-style match between Europe and Great Britain played at Sunningdale. I played four times, winning two out of three in the pairs and then beat Ian Woosnam 4 and 3. I started with an eagle and was out in 29 to set up the victory. Having played in the Hennessey Cup at the beginning of my career, it was fun to see the event reintroduced.

While I had not won for three years I felt that I was not far away. Since the win in the German Masters in October 1997, I had finished second five times. Perhaps 2001 would be my year again.

Chapter 14

Payne Stewart

On 25 October 1999, Payne Stewart stood on the steps of his home and blew kisses to his wife and children. Later that day he died in an aeroplane tragedy. He was the reigning US Open Golf Champion.

At forty-two, Payne was in the prime of life, and had had a great year winning the US Open and playing on the victorious US Ryder Cup team. Over the previous year or two Payne had undergone a transformation, a renewal of his Christian faith – signified by the WWJD (what would Jesus do) bracelet he wore, a gift from his young son. He had begun to re-examine his faith and strengthen it after observing how his friend and fellow golfer Paul Azinger was sustained by his faith during his battle with cancer.

When I heard the news I was playing in the Volvo Masters at Montecastillo in Spain. Everybody was in shock. We could not believe how his life had been snuffed out like that. We all felt for Tracey and the kids. All the players were stunned. We decided that we should honour him in some way. We had a players' meeting and it was agreed that we should have a get-together before or after play next day and one of us should say a few words as a tribute to him.

I thought that Ken Schofield as executive director of the tour should do it, but they all seemed to be pointing at me and I was happy to do it. So we met at the eighteenth green and honoured Payne for the kind of person he was, the player but also the friend. We knew we were going to miss him in the future. I finished my tribute with these words, 'Payne, we will miss you but we know you've gone to a better place to be with your heavenly Father.' Amen.

I have lots of great memories of Payne. He was a musician and played in a band called 'Jake Trout and the Flounders' with Peter Jacobson and one or two others. They sometimes played at tournaments. He had a very outgoing personality.

Even the way he dressed was different, with his colourful plus-fours. He wasn't the kind of guy that you would miss if he was around. He always stood out – not just from the way he dressed but also by his personality. He was very competitive but at the same time always treated everyone well. He was a lot of fun to be with.

I played against him in three Ryder Cups. He was as competitive and patriotic as anyone, yet the way he acted in the 1999 singles with Colin Montgomerie was typical of the man. Colin was subjected to some disgraceful barracking by the US crowd. Payne first remonstrated with the gallery. Then when the outcome of the Ryder Cup was already settled and the Montgomerie/Stewart match was the last one on the course, Payne Stewart conceded the final hole and the match to his opponent.

At the funeral service in Orlando, Paul Azinger told two stories about Payne. In one tournament Paul just beat Payne. Payne congratulated him, and told the press how well Paul had played. Then when Azinger went to the locker room to change he found Payne had filled his shoes with banana!

Paul and Payne used to go fishing together and Payne got a new boat of which he was so proud. One day he went into his garage and started up the motor just to enjoy the sensation. He started revving up the engine until suddenly the engine blew up. Payne had not realised that the motor needed to be in water to operate safely.

As Paul Azinger told the packed congregation in First Baptist Church in Orlando, Payne made two mistakes. 'First, he blew up the engine and, second, he told me about it. I told everyone!' At the next tournament Paul stuck on Payne's locker a picture of an engine for a boat with the caption, 'Just add water.'

Paul also quoted these words from the Bible: 'I have fought well I have finished the race and I have been faithful. So a crown of righteousness will be given to me for pleasing the Lord.' He added, 'Payne Stewart finished the race and was faithful. Now the crown of righteousness is his.'

At the funeral service they also played an extract from a TV interview for a national golf show recorded a couple of weeks before in which Payne had talked about the future. He said, 'I am going to a special place when I die, but I want to make sure that my life is special while I'm here.' It is great that he was ready to go. I know I will see him in heaven.

Chapter 15

Money – the 'root of all evil'?

People sometimes ask me, how can I live as a Christian yet have so much money? There is no doubt that I am a wealthy man. My earnings from golf are public knowledge as they are in the newspapers and golf magazines every month. I cannot deny that I have made a lot of money from my profession. I have certain gifts and talents and I'm blessed that they earn a lot of money. Other people have different talents and work just as hard but do not earn so much.

This is in total contrast to my early life where we did not have money. As I said, as a child, most of my clothes were hand-me-downs from my older brother. For many years I hardly had anything new. The irony is that, at that stage, I wanted clothes and couldn't afford them. Now, when I can afford to buy anything I want, I have contracts with clothing companies – for example, for sixteen years with Hugo Boss and now with Lacoste – and not only get the clothes free, but I am actually paid to wear them!

Having experienced both poverty and riches, I think my attitude to money is balanced. Money is a necessary evil. I don't need a lot of money, but it doesn't hurt having it either. There's nothing wrong with being rich as long as you don't make money your god. Sometimes, though, it can be a difficult path to walk, especially nowadays because people have become so materialistic. Many people make money their first priority.

I really never needed a lot of money to be happy. I'm not a money person. I don't go out and buy a new Porsche or a Mercedes when I win a tournament. I don't need that sort of thing. One of the best things about having money is I can travel first class, stay in the best hotels and don't have to penny-pinch. Travelling is a big part of my life. I am away from home more than half the year. The job I do requires me to be physically and mentally prepared for my day's work.

I remember in the first few years when I didn't have any money, how tough it was to travel, to spend ten hours in a car and then get out and try to play in a golf tournament. Or to fly ten hours on the back seat of a plane so you're so stiff you can't move for three days.

The Bible says that God will bless us abundantly. Jesus said, 'I have come so that you will have life in all its fulness.' That doesn't necessarily have to mean money. It could mean being blessed and rich in other ways, but I think it includes money. If you read in the Bible the accounts of King David or King Solomon, God blessed them with tremendous wealth. Again there is the story of Job. We read that God made him one of the richest people alive.

The Bible also says 'It is easier for a camel to go through the eye of a needle than for a rich man to enter the kingdom of God.' When I first read this, it did not make any sense to me, so I asked Larry Moody, the PGA tour chaplain, 'Does this mean no rich man can ever get into heaven?'

He explained that the eye of the needle referred to a walled city with a very narrow gate and a large gate. At night they closed the large gate and a camel could squeeze through the small gate but it had to be unloaded and to bend down.

So it means that the rich man can get to heaven but it's just that much harder. What Jesus is really referring to with this verse is that most people get rich because they put money before God and you shouldn't put anything before God. You shouldn't have any idols and money can be an idol, as it is to a lot of people nowadays.

My children grow up in a wealthy family and I find that a real challenge. When I was a child we had very little. Now, within reason, I can afford for my children to have anything they want so their experience is totally different from mine. I really try to instil into them the value of money. I try to make them think how they spend their money and help them not to buy things they want just because they have the money. I also try to teach them the concept of being stewards, that their money is a gift from God and that, for example, when we go to church, they should give some of their money back to God.

I recognise too that I have responsibility for the money I have. The more I make, the more I can give away to charity and other good causes. I have also always been aware that it is not my money but that I am just a steward, taking care of God's money. I try not to waste it by spending it on things I don't need. I believe I am accountable to God for what I have done with my money.

As I say, the more I make, the more there is to give away. I never talk about what I give because, as it says in the Bible, if you tell others about it you've already received your reward on earth and so will not receive it in heaven. So if I'm going to boast about how much money I give away then I've already received my reward here. I don't want that.

Some temptations come with money – you have to be sure that you have your priorities right and that you don't do things just for money. But I have found that the more money I have, the less important it becomes to me. Some other people say the more they have the more they want but that is not how I feel.

I'm sure that God does not say anywhere that you ought to be poor, or you can't have money, or you can't be successful in what you are doing. He's the one who gave us our talents.

He gave me the talent to play golf so well; it wasn't my own doing. Sure, I have to work hard and use those talents to the best of my ability, but if he hadn't given them to me I wouldn't be where I am.

A journalist once asked me, if my house was on fire and everyone was safely out, which one thing would I want to retrieve? I couldn't think of anything. I'm not a materialistic person; there's nothing in my house I couldn't live without.

For me, happiness is having people around me who are family, people I love and care for. And knowing God. All the other things are just material things. I enjoy having a good car but cars rust eventually and when you die you can't take any of these material things with you.

The hardest thing about the lifestyle of the tournament golfer is the travel, being away from home so much. Jet-lag becomes a way of life. It isn't like a businessman who is away for two or three days. I tend to be away for two or three weeks at a time. I feel that I have missed so many things in my kids' lives – taking their first steps, saying first words and so on. I have missed so many birthdays.

At the moment I play about twenty-five to twenty-seven tournaments each year, and Vikki is probably with me for no more than five. In the Florida tournaments, she may come for the weekends, but it is all totally different from the period when she would be out with me most weeks. I long to have a bit more time at home.

The lifestyle of the golfer puts a lot of pressure on a marriage when one is away so much. Vikki sometimes talks about getting into the 'mode' of me not being there. It is as though we live two separate lives – a life together and a life apart – and it takes time to adjust from one to the other.

I know that when I am away on my own I live a more selfish lifestyle. Everything revolves around me. I have more time to do the things I want to do. When I am home I try to be a servant to the family, to be available, to help, to be part of their lives. It is the same for Vikki – when I am away, she has to be responsible for everything. When I am home, I can help her with all that.

We now have four children – Jackie (born 1986), Stefan (1990), Christina (1993) and Jason (2000). Being a parent is a very demanding and rewarding activity. It certainly is a challenge. It is a wonderful thing that we are blessed with and I would miss not having kids. I believe parents should spend time with their kids and teach them everything.

Our children have grown up in an unusual environment, having travelled the world since they were babies. I think they have gained from my lifestyle. It is a great privilege for them to have travelled so much and to have seen so much of the world. Seeing different countries, different people, different customs perhaps makes you more rounded and with a better understanding of the world. I myself feel that I have gained so much from my travels, learning where countries are, what money they use, what food they eat and so on.

One thing we learned was that in Spain, for example, it is impossible to get food at 6.00 p.m. They don't eat dinner in Spain until nine or ten at night. So if you are trying to get your kids dinner so you can get them to bed early, it isn't possible in Spain.

Sometimes there can be tensions when the family is at a tournament. If I feel I have a problem and need to spend an hour hitting balls to sort it out, they may not understand why I don't seem to want to see them. They may think, 'You have finished your round, forget about golf. Come out with us.' We usually compromise and sometimes being told to forget about golf for the evening may be just what I need to hear.

The neat thing is that the kids – especially when they were younger – really don't mind if I have shot 65 or 75; they still want to spend time with me. I also sometimes have to make an effort not to take my mood with me and to leave the 75 behind when I go out to dinner with the family. That isn't always easy.

Because I am German and Vikki is American, the kids are exposed to two languages and two cultures. Even though we are living in the USA, I really want the kids to maintain their links with Germany and to continue to speak German, which they all speak – some better than others. The two older kids were born in Germany and the two younger ones in the USA. They all have dual citizenship. They can decide at a later stage which they want to be.

Generally speaking, the children enjoy spending half the year in Germany and half in the USA. Sometimes when we go to Germany they enjoy it so much that they are sorry to have to leave and come back to America. I think they see the good and the bad in both Germany and the USA. It has been good for them to be exposed to both cultures.

I have always enjoyed being in the USA and found it easy to adjust. I think it is much easier to get to know people in the USA than in Europe. In Germany you call people 'Mr' or 'Mrs' until you know them quite well. In the USA, it is first name from the start. Sometimes Vikki has a harder time in Germany because her German isn't so good and she finds it harder to be involved in conversations.

When I am home I try to be available for the kids from 3 p.m. I pick them up from school and I try to be around to drive them where they need to go, to watch Jackie play football (or soccer as it is called in America), to play golf with Stefan, to help Vikki around the house – just to be a normal Dad.

One or two weeks a year we try to go off skiing and we all enjoy it. They all ski pretty well. As a family we like doing sports together, such as skating, bowling, cycling, basketball or football. We all enjoy being outdoors.

In school they all do sport. This year Jackie has been playing football for the school team, Christina is very much into gymnastics and Stefan has become very keen on golf. I enjoy playing golf with Stefan – whether playing a round or just practising. Jackie has played a bit of golf and Christina sometimes hits balls but neither of them is very interested.

We love to play board-games – Monopoly, Risk or whatever – in the evenings or at weekends. Unfortunately I am still very competitive even in board-games, and will never let the kids win unless they beat me fair and square. I try to control it but my natural instinct is to want to do well in everything I do. If I have the edge in the game I try to help the kids to understand my strategies so that they will do better next time.

I think it is important to try to eat breakfast and dinner together. It is just a great way to spend twenty minutes or half an hour together, to talk and to catch up with each other. We have a short Bible reading and prayer together as a family at breakfast.

Because I am on the road for most of the year, I miss out on regular church attendance. When I am home for a few weeks I like to get involved in a Bible study group – where we study the Bible and do some homework to prepare for the next study.

Vikki and I try to have one night out together each week. We go out to dinner or for a walk on the beach, but lately we have found a church in Fort Lauderdale where there is a great preacher. We go there on a Saturday evening and then have dinner afterwards. So that is our date. We really enjoy it.

While the kids are in school we like to go out to lunch or for walks. There is a nice three-mile walk around where we live. That is where we catch up and talk about decisions we have to make. When I am home I go to the gym and work out four or five times a week for an hour and a half. I love all sports so I take the opportunity to play tennis, and I enjoy watching all the sports on TV.

* * *

At first when I started to win tournaments, I thought I could be a famous golfer as well as a private person, but it doesn't work like that. People think they have a right to talk to you at any time, to interrupt you, ask you for an autograph when you are trying to have a quiet dinner with the family. I had to adjust my life to deal with this. Eventually, I came to the conclusion that it was better to have this pressure as it meant I was popular and doing well. They say that worse than having to sign autographs is never being asked! On balance, fame and the loss of some of your privacy is the lesser of two evils.

Each day I get from ten to twenty requests for autographs in the mail. That is not a lot, but if I have been away for three weeks it is quite a pile. I have a secretary who sorts it all out for me but she can't sign them for me! I spend more time in my office than I want to but somebody has to do it.

There are times when you don't want to talk to people, perhaps times when you have been away and just want to have a private dinner with your wife. Sometimes I go somewhere to spend time with my kids – like going to hit balls with my son. Every two minutes somebody comes along for an autograph, to talk about last week's tournament, the Ryder Cup or whatever.

Because I am a celebrity people think they can interrupt and that can be frustrating. I am used to it but it is difficult for the family who may just want some normal family time. I don't want to be rude to anyone, but if I have told Stefan that I will spend an hour watching him hitting balls and teaching him, that is what I want to do – not talk to strangers.

Perhaps this is the most difficult thing – this demand on my time. Because I am already away from the family so much, I want to give them my time when I am at home. But when we go out somewhere together we can find it impossible to be just normal people. The press can also be intrusive. I realise they have their job to do and I try to accommodate them, but I can be asked to give interviews time and time again – I am happy to do it but it takes up a lot of my time.

When I succeed in getting the balance right it is good for the family but it is also good for my golf. Keeping it in perspective is a major reason why I have been able to keep going well into my forties, still playing at this level. I have not lost the fun of playing golf and I have not lost the drive to do well.

Getting the balance between my work, my family and God is the challenge I strive for.

Chapter 16

Moving to the USA

In 1984 I played a few tournaments in the USA and did well enough to earn my card to play on the US tour the following year. Up to that point I had only thought of playing the European tour. Now I had another option.

I played enough tournaments in the USA for the next few years to keep my playing rights in the USA but still played the majority of the European season. In 1984 I married Vikki, who is American. That also changed my perspective on playing in the USA. We bought a house in Florida and developed the pattern of spending the summer in Europe and the winter in the USA.

We continued that pattern as our children were born. We also took the decision that the children would go to school in the USA. That is not quite as straightforward as it sounds, as we did full home-schooling and also partial home-schooling.

With Jackie, our oldest, we also had a compromise with her attending school but home-schooling at the beginning and end of the year. The school accommodated this arrangement, which meant that we could spend six months in Europe and six months in the USA. That was great because we wanted to be in the USA for the winter anyway.

The family travelled with me and used the hotel for school while I was working. There was a little friction and some problems but generally it worked. Certainly it was better than being separated for long periods – the lesser of two evils, really.

But when Christina, our third child, was of school age it became too difficult to home-school the three of them, all at different stages. When Jackie was approaching high-school age we felt it was time to stop and let her settle down into normal school life like everyone else. It wasn't fair on her to be pulled out of school for two months at the beginning and end of the year.

We were trying to balance two things and it wasn't easy. I had to follow my career around Europe, the USA and occasionally beyond. At the same time I did not want to be separated from the family for long periods. Thus we developed the pattern of my trying to be in the USA when the children were in school and the family travelling with me when I was in Europe.

At that stage I did all the travelling, playing two or three events in Europe and then coming back for one or two weeks with the family and then off again. But that was not really what I wanted to do, so it was an easy decision to stay in the USA to play. I am sure it was the right decision for all involved for me to play and spend more time in the USA.

In 2001 I decided to rejoin the US tour and adopted a pattern of playing about seventeen tournaments in the USA, with twelve in Europe. To keep my tour memberships, I have to play fifteen tournaments in the USA and eleven in Europe. However, it is a bit more complicated than that, since the major tournaments count for both tours. But equally, there are some tournaments I play, such as Sun City and other invitational events, which don't count for either tour.

In 2001 I also officially moved my residence to America – which is significant for tax purposes and the number of days I can stay in the USA. As I said, the main reason for the move was the children's schooling and spending more time with the family.

* * *

As far as playing in the USA is concerned, I enjoy it for several reasons. Overall the courses are better than in Europe, the greens are faster, prize money is higher and the competition is stronger. I see all those as advantages.

Having played the European tour for so long, one thing that I enjoy about the USA is going to different places that I haven't seen before. At times the European tour felt like 'Same city, same golf course, same hotel'.

Having said that, many new courses are being developed in Europe and some of them are more American than traditional European. We used not to have irrigation; now we have water everywhere. More and more courses have rough around the greens, just like courses on the US tour. That makes chipping and pitching different. It is certainly changing.

For a player, the difference between the US and the European tours is like the difference between a five-star and a three-star hotel. In the USA you get a courtesy car every week. I fly into the city of the tournament, I am met and provided with a car, which is mine for the week. That is very nice. The tour also provides me with a cellphone and a computer.

A more important difference is at the golf course itself. In the USA the practice facilities are always extremely good, compared to Europe. The greens are faster and better. Some courses in Europe have great greens but, equally, many are very average.

The locker room is much more spacious and you have your own locker every week. There is food set up in the locker room, whereas in many tournaments in Europe the players have to eat in public restaurants. This means that if you want, you can have a quick snack and be out again in ten minutes – which often would not be possible at a European tournament.

Quite simply, the difference is that in the USA the sponsors and tournament organisers want to do everything to make the players feel comfortable and want to come back. In Europe, it often seems to me that the tournament looks after the sponsors and their guests far more than the players.

The money is much better in America, with the prize money at a typical tournament twice what it is in Europe. At the moment the US tour is more international, with the best players coming from around the world competing. I enjoy the extra competition and the opportunity of playing against the best players, week in week out.

In the USA you have much more of the feeling of being part of a big event – even if it is just a routine tournament. In Europe there are some great tournaments, but some where you play with hardly any spectators and not much TV coverage. There is so much more atmosphere on the US tour.

The USA is the centre of world golf. All the new equipment, new clubs and new balls come out of the USA and reach Europe perhaps several months later. The US market is just so much bigger. The USA is a good place for the professional golfer to be based.

Chapter 17

What makes me tick?

What is my greatest strength as a golfer? It is difficult to sit back and analyse and assess myself, but I will try. I would say that my greatest strength is not having a particular weakness – although all my game could, of course, be better. At my best I am straight off the tee, good with the irons, good out of the bunker and a solid putter. I am not the best at any of these but pretty good overall. My total package is built on good technique, a good short game, mental strength, good preparation, good course management, fitness and lots of family support.

As I get older and as the game develops, perhaps my length off the tee is a weakness. There are now quite a number of players who can hit the ball forty or fifty yards past me. That puts pressure on me. I have to hit my approach shots with great precision.

Consistency is also a key word in my profile. Twice in Europe I have played fifty consecutive tournaments without missing a cut. In the golden years, when I was not winning tournaments I was still in contention most weeks.

I've never had a problem with determination or setting goals. First I try to beat myself, then I beat the course and eventually the others. I've always paced myself – I don't play week after week. I play for a couple of weeks then take one off, which I've done for years now.

Course management and golf-course strategy has always been a strong part of my game. By that I mean the way I approach the course and attack the hole. Playing the right shot is crucial. Knowing when to go for the pin and when to play safe can save a lot of shots. I feel that I have a good understanding of my own game, which is a real help.

I am said to be particularly good in bad weather though I don't know why that should be. Part of it may be my attitude. I don't go out there screaming at the weather – how would that help anyway? I accept what happens, whether it is windy or not. If you think positively and keep your mind on what's right, it gives you a better attitude. If you moan and groan and are disgusted, you play miserably too.

Mentally I am very strong, so most of the problems I have are technical. My swing may go wrong and I cannot fix it right away. Not many of us have perfect swings so we have compensatory moves. So when they go slightly off, everything is off. I have had the same coach for virtually all my professional career and we still work as hard at improving my game as we did fifteen years ago.

I think too that I am a very positive person. We all have a tendency to dwell on the bad things. I try to focus more on the good things. I think the only way to improve ourselves and our lives is to look at the positive side and not dwell on the past. In fact the Bible says, 'Whatever is true, whatever is noble, whatever is right, whatever is pure, whatever is lovely, whatever is admirable, think about such things.'

We often get so anxious about everything; we have too many fears and anxieties in our lives, which hold us back. I have learnt that when I try to figure everything out myself, there are too many things that are not under my control. But if they are out of my control, then it is pointless to worry about them. It is better if I leave them to God and put my energy into what I can control.

Another challenge is not to leave shots on the course.

Throughout the years this is something I have worked on. Peter Kostis, the golf coach, says that on any given day you have a range of scores, say 67 to 71. That means if I take all my chances, I shoot 67. If I make a few mistakes and leave shots on the course, I shoot 71.

It used to be one of my greatest strengths that I didn't leave any shots out on the course, and in a period such as 1998–2000 when I didn't win, the difference was the number of shots I left out there. In 2001 I felt that I was back to not leaving shots on the course and making the best of the opportunities that I created.

Everyone can hit bad drives. The difference is whether you get it up and down to save par or if you play another bad shot and finish with a double or triple bogey.

Sometimes I get annoyed on the golf course. I'm no saint. You see, that's a common misunderstanding – people think that just because you're a Christian then you are going to be all holy. I still sin just as much as anybody; I'm not like God. I'm trying to be more like him, but I'm always falling short.

I would never get upset with another player or anyone else. The problem is with me. If you can beat the golf course, and yourself, you have a good chance to win.

When something goes wrong on the course, I have learnt that it is best for me to get over it as soon as possible. It is history. I cannot change it. I didn't do it deliberately to harm myself. I had good intentions but could not pull it off. You need to learn to forgive yourself and to do it quickly.

There was a time when I used to get angry with myself and call myself names for an hour or so. The result was that I just made more bogeys, and that doesn't do you any good. Now I try to get mad at myself for a minute for two and get it out of my system. By the time of the next shot I need to be over it and ready to focus on the shot I am going to play – but it doesn't always work that way.

Perhaps I don't worry as much about things as some people because I realise that they are really out of my control anyway, a lot of the time. I just try to give many things over to God. All I can do is the best I can possibly do but ultimately what the outcome will be is in his hands; then it is easy to forgive myself because I am trying the best I can and I can't do more than that.

It is an interesting fact that I have won three times during the week after the Ryder Cup – including the week after Kiawah Island and That Putt. There is no explanation for that but perhaps I am better than some players at leaving the past behind. I know some people who can remember every incident in their career. I'm not like that – I often say that I live in the future, not in the past.

Part of this is having a range of interests so that you are not just focused on golf, golf, golf. Everyone should have one mad ambition. Mine is to win a downhill ski race! I have always enjoyed skiing and I ski every year. I suppose I am a two- or three-handicap skier. I would like to ski more but there is always the risk of a broken bone so I only go around Christmas when there would be a few months to recover before the first major, should anything happen. I enjoy the beauty of the mountains and trees and the icicles and just the different environment. I love nature.

Are top sportspeople born or made? A bit of both, I would say. Obviously, I have been blessed with a reasonable amount of natural ability and I have worked hard to develop and exploit that talent to the full. I have also had to have the character to see me through hard times. I have experienced the despair of watching my putting stroke all but disintegrate before my eyes, and then the satisfaction of recovering from this ordeal – not once, but three times!

I am fortunate that I have always enjoyed practice. I go out and hit balls almost every day I am home – which a lot of my colleagues don't do any more. Some people find it boring and want to play all the time, but I don't mind practice. I enjoy trying new things, trying to improve. I am often working on a particular aspect of my swing just to make me a better player.

Although I hit balls most days, my practice routine is different every day, depending on what I want to accomplish and the time I have available. For example, I might hit balls for half an hour to an hour. I might work on the short game for half an hour and I might play a few holes.

When hitting balls I would start with the sand wedge and work my way up. I don't hit every club – perhaps the sand wedge, the eight, the five and the three and then the woods. I would never hit every club in the bag.

When I am preparing for a major, sometimes I play a tournament the week before and sometimes I take the week off to practise at home. You never know which is better. In 2002, for example, I played seven weeks in a row in February/ March so I took two weeks off before the Masters. I felt I needed the break. Other times if you haven't played for a bit, you feel you need to play to get back into the swing of things. For me it depends on what I have done over the previous month and how I am feeling.

Part of my practice time is testing new clubs or balls. That takes up many hours. That is partly for the benefit of the manufacturer of the equipment but it is beneficial for me if I find a club that works better than the old one. Similarly Strata will send me three new types of ball to test. If one of them works better that the one I am currently using, that helps me too.

Some mornings you wake up and it's pouring with rain, freezing cold and blowing a gale, and you don't really want to go out and play golf. Fortunately there are not too many days like that – especially if you spend the winter in Florida. Most of the time I'm happy with my job and happy being out there, enjoying myself – even if it might not look like it at times.

There are not many people I would want to swap with. I'd rather be out on a golf course than sitting in an office for eight hours at a stretch.

Like everybody, I have days when everything feels awful and I wonder if it's ever going to get right again. It may not be just days, it sometimes lasts for weeks if I get into a slump and just can't see the light at the end of the tunnel.

In times like these, my belief in God has helped me a great deal. Because I have other priorities in my life now, golf is not everything any more. Sadly many people don't have that and I wish they would; I can see them suffer through it.

Prayer is another key to my life. Prayer is talking to God, and is something I do every day. Some people think you have to go to church to pray but you can pray anywhere. I pray on the golf course and I pray about anything and everything. It doesn't necessarily have to be about golf. It can be far removed or it can be part of the moment too. In the morning when I get up, in the first few minutes, I usually give over my whole day to God. I concentrate and meditate on God and what he wants me to do and what he wants me to be, and the day also ends that way too. And during the day I spend several moments praying and just focusing on him.

I sometimes pray between shots. After I have hit a shot I have anywhere from two to five minutes until we come to the next one, and during that time I can pray or thank him for the many blessings he has given me, or for the people he has brought into my life. There are many things I can thank him for and I use the time for that.

I am much more thankful than I used to be. I always thought, 'I'm the one in charge, I am the boss. I can do it all myself.' The older I get the more I realise that is not the case. Whatever I have can be taken away in a few seconds or a few days, and events can happen where you lose everything you have and more. So I rely much more on him and I trust him that he will provide for me; and I just try to be more like him, which isn't always easy.

Before I was a Christian I prayed in church or maybe before lunch and dinner and before I went to bed. But nowadays I can pray anywhere, at any given time, whether it's between shots on the golf course, driving a car or just wherever I am. My understanding of prayer is quite different now. I'm learning to give my whole day over to the Lord each morning. I ask him to lead me and help me to treat other people in a loving and honourable way – to help me deal with the daily frustrations of life.

Even though I grew up as an altar boy in the church, I never had my own Bible until I went to the tour Bible study in 1985. Reading the Bible is another important part of my life. The Bible is a humongous book; there is so much wisdom and truth in it. It is God's word, and I read it to learn about him and be what he wants me to be.

With the Bible you learn different lessons every time you pick it up. There's so much in there; it's like a handbook for life. When you buy a car or even a refrigerator you get a manual on how to use it. The Bible is the manual for life.

It says in the Bible, 'Meditate on my word day and night.' That means all the time – or as often as you can. Sometimes I write a few verses down and carry them around with me. Usually when I play late, I have some time in the morning to read the Bible and make a few notes.

I live my life without fear. Death does not scare me. I believe that Jesus died and rose again and that I have eternal life. All of us are going to die at some stage. I believe that we are in the world of the dying, going to the world of the living and not the other way round. When I die, I know that I will go to heaven to be with God for ever. If you don't know what will happen to you when you die, that must be a source of anxiety and a burden to carry.

147

Of course there are things I don't understand. For example, why is there so much suffering in the world? Why do evil people sometimes seem to have a better life than good people? But when you look at it from an eternal perspective – and God is eternal – it's totally different. This life doesn't mean all that much when you look at it from an eternal perspective. What are these seventy or eighty years that we live here compared to the millions and billions of years of eternity? I think we put too much emphasis on ourselves, we are too selfish. Like when you make a three-putt and you throw a temper tantrum. There are far more important things going on in the world than a three-putt. This helps me keep things in perspective.

People say I don't smile much on the course. I am not really aware of that. They say I constantly concentrate, which is not true. You couldn't concentrate for four and a half hours in a row – no way. I wish I could smile more and be a bit more happy and outgoing, but it's probably not me and you've got to be yourself.

I am sometimes amazed at the way some of my colleagues play practice rounds because they just seem to wander along and chat to each other and never even look at the course. I'm out there making mental notes and writing things down, making mental pictures of what the course looks like. This is something that I think is a very important part of my tournament week.

From all this I derive my game plan and how to attack a certain hole. That can make a huge difference. If you play the same course, year after year, you don't have to spend so much detail on preparation, but I can't believe some players who don't take the time to take in the details.

Peter and I will be out there, sometimes with three or four different drivers, trying one and then another to get the best one for the tournament. Apparently the caddie, Dave Musgove, said that playing a practice round on my own, I could hold up a four-ball. That is an exaggeration but I do like to be meticulous in my preparation. Confidence is vital to a professional sportsman. For me confidence starts with good preparation and lots of practice.

There is a story that Peter once told me it was 150 yards to the flag from a sprinkler head. I am supposed to have replied, 'Front of the sprinkler head or back?' It is a good story but it isn't true – as far as I know Colin Montgomerie made it up. It was when we were playing together in the Ryder Cup and he was listening to my conversations with Peter. I am precise about my distances but not quite that precise!

I always like to be prepared. When a situation happens in a tournament, you are under pressure and you only have so much time to make up your mind. So I want to have all the information I possibly can about the distance and layout of the hole, and I take a lot of time in the practice rounds to gather precise yardages and distances so that I don't have to guess or calculate things during the tournament.

As I reach my mid-forties, I am often asked what keeps me going. That is a good question. If I retired now I would probably not need to work any more. But I love the competition, I love the game of golf and I like to win. Those three factors keep me going.

It's always exciting to be in the lead or near the lead with a chance of winning on Sunday. It gets the adrenaline going. Maybe the very first time was more special because I had never experienced it before, but I know that I'll be just as excited as I ever was if I am leading in my next tournament.

I still enjoy the competition as much as ever and that motivates me to work out, to keep fit and to practise. Playing golf in a competitive environment has been such a big part of my life that I would miss it if I stopped.

Part of the motivation to making the cut is that if I didn't, I would make myself spend the weekend practising and trying to work out what went wrong, in order to be able to do better next time. It is more fun to play.

The world of professional golf is a very selfish and competitive life. As an individual sport, golf is probably more selfish than a professional team sport. Even though we all get along well on the tour and many of the other players are my personal friends, the bottom line is a selfish one. I am out there to win and to beat all the others – day in, day out. Sometimes you are happy when one of your friends wins, but you would still be trying 100 per cent to beat them.

I gain a tremendous amount of mental strength through my belief in God. It may be hard for a non-believer to understand and to relate to what I am saying, and I recognise, too, that for a lot of readers this may all sound like a bunch of baloney. However, if you want to know the secret of what I have achieved in golf over a long career and how I remain competitive into my mid-forties, then this is a large part of it.

I am not saying that I win tournaments because I am a Christian. I became a believer in 1985 when I was already successful and a Masters champion. However, I have had seventeen good years since. I personally believe that my faith has played a big part in keeping me going and giving me such longevity.

However bad things get, my belief tells me I am important in God's eyes. That makes me feel good. It stops my self-esteem dropping when I have just hit a bad shot or a bad putt. When I missed the putt in the Ryder Cup in Kiawah Island in 1991 and when I spent months struggling with the yips, my belief helped me put things in perspective. Before 1985, golf was everything in my life. Now golf is just a part of it and I know that if golf was taken away from me, I could still be a happy person.

For some people, golf is too important to them. I look at some of my colleagues and I see that golf is all-consuming for them. If they cannot perform to the level that they want to – and none of us can consistently – they are miserable and their whole life is in danger of falling apart. That could well have happened to me if it were not for my relationship with God. I still like to win and it is still important for me to do well, but perhaps it is not as all-consuming as it used to be for me.

I know that God loves me whether I shoot 80 or 60. He always will and he will forgive me for my mistakes as long as I feel sorry for them. That is a tremendous asset in my life. We all have a certain amount of guilt that we walk around with and we know we have done things that we should not have done. If you don't have God's forgiveness, it must be a tremendous burden to walk around with.

One of my mottoes in life is to try to treat everyone the way I would want to be treated myself. At the beginning of my career I found the media difficult to deal with. I wasn't used to being in the newspapers. I once allowed a journalist to caddie for me, knowing that he was going to write a story afterwards. But I was just devastated by what he wrote. He said I was throwing clubs, doing this and doing that. I just asked myself, 'Where is he getting this from? He has been with me for five days and has seen everything I did. Why did he make all this up?'

Or I may take an hour of my time to give a personal interview to someone and then two days later I read it. I know that what I said is totally different from what he has written in the newspaper. He has put words in my mouth that I didn't say. I sometimes wonder why I wasted my time talking to him when I could have done something better with my time. I could have let him make up things about me and write them without giving my time – because that's what he did anyway.

But that doesn't work either. You cannot ignore journalists so you've got to find a way to live with them. On the whole I think I've managed to maintain good relationships with most of the golf journalists. You have to recognise, too, that some people work for newspapers that only want the negative and sensational stuff, so they have to write like that or lose their job.

There have been occasions when I thought that something about me in the press was unfair and untrue. When the press write about you, sometimes the truth is not sellable, so they make up stuff, but there's not much I can do about that. I just try to avoid these people. And since I've become a Christian I try to forgive them. It's not easy but I've been able to do that.

It is my relationship with God that keeps my perspective and my priorities right. I honestly don't know how people make it through life without God.

I have shared with you the ups and downs of my golf career. I have also shared with you my faith in God and the difference that makes to my life. I am not asking you to take what I am saying as true. Get yourself a Bible and look into it and find out whether Jesus Christ really lived, whether there is a God, or if there is any alternative. I am convinced that Christianity is true and that this whole world would be a much more peaceful and loving place if we started respecting each other and loving each other like Jesus told us to.

Chapter 18

Great golfers

During my career I have had the privilege of playing with and against all the great players of the modern era. In this chapter I want to reflect on a few players that I admire. It is hard to start with anyone but Tiger Woods.

Since Tiger turned professional he has taken the golf world by storm. He has established himself firmly as the world's number one player and has already won over thirty events in the US, including eight majors.

It is amazing how much impact on the game of golf Tiger has had. I feel very positive about it all. All the hype surrounding him has given golf another push in the right direction. It has made golf interesting to those who maybe did not follow the game before, and people will come who just want to watch him, which is great for the game of golf.

I have also been impressed with what he has said. Although he is relatively young he has shown great maturity. I can think of a lot of other young players who have made some stupid comments, but Tiger has avoided those mistakes. I think he is a great role model.

I know he is making a great deal of money, but I think it is good for all of us as we have a chance to win it as well. Some of the increases in prize money are due to him. Through him, the game has risen to a new level of popularity it has never had before – not only in the USA but also worldwide.

Whenever he is in the field, there are more spectators, more interest, more TV viewers and more people on the course – just more of everything.

People sometimes ask if I like playing with Tiger or if there are too many distractions. I have played with him perhaps ten times and I always enjoy it. He is good to play with. He is very intense, but a real gentleman. Of course there is a lot of hoop-la and cheering but I enjoy the added excitement and atmosphere. The only problem is, if he has finished the hole the gallery is rushing off to the next tee while you still have a three-footer to finish. Then it can be difficult not to be distracted. But that happened with Seve and Arnold too.

Tiger is an exceptional golfer. In his short career he has already broken many records. He has set the standard and it is up to the rest of us to match him and knock him off the pedestal, and then we will deserve the attention. As a player I don't resent Tiger at all. In my opinion what he has done has been very positive.

Tiger really does not have a weakness. It all starts from his physique. He has a body that is strong and flexible. That is a wonderful combination that not many of us have. He had obviously worked on that but he has been blessed with good genes as well.

He has a very good technique. Everyone knows that he can hit the ball a great distance but he can spin the ball a lot as well. He also has a tremendous touch around the greens. When you add to his distance that he is one of the best chippers and pitchers in the game, you can see why he scores so well. He can also be a lethal putter. Didn't he win the putting statistics as well one year? When you combine a great driver with a brilliant short game and putting, then you are bound to win tournaments.

On top of this ability, he is determined and one of the hardest working players. He just wants to be the best and to break all the records.

* * *

In Europe, Seve was the charismatic character who helped lift European golf to a new level, with three wins in the Open Championship plus a US Masters. I have had a great rivalry with Seve over the years. We were both trying to be the dominant player in Europe. We went head to head many times. The play-off for the Lancôme in 1986 in a way summed up the rivalry between us. After four holes we were still level and it was getting dark so we gave up, halved the match and shared the prize.

Seve and I are the same age but he was already an established player and major winner by the time I won my first tournament. We had a period of time from about 1981 right through to the early 1990s when we were competing for everything. A lot of tournaments were decided between us.

Seve was a good ball-striker with a great short game. He had all the shots and was a great putter. But his greatest strength was his imagination in the range of shots he could come up with. He was incredible the way he could play recovery shots. Just when you thought you had him, he would produce an unbelievable shot to save par. With Seve it was never over until it was over.

He is very competitive and one of the best matchplayers who has ever lived. It is no surprise to me that he has won the World Matchplay at Wentworth five times. He beat me in it more than once.

I admire Nick Faldo a lot. He had won, I think, three tournaments in one year, but could not do what he wanted to in the majors so he decided to remodel his entire swing. He basically gave up almost two years of his career to remodel everything – of course, with no guarantee that it would work. It wasn't that he was playing badly but just that he wanted to get to the next level and was prepared to gamble to achieve it.

But when he had finished, Nick started winning majors and

finished up with three Open Championships and three US Masters titles and became a dominant player on the world stage for a few years. What he did was very brave. I don't think I could be that brave to sacrifice two or three years hopefully to get where I wanted to be with no assurance of success.

Sandy Lyle topped the money list in Europe three times and also won the Open Championship and the US Masters. He could hit the ball a really long way. In pure distance he was up with John Daly and even Tiger. I have never seen anyone who could hit a one or two iron as far or as high as Sandy.

Ian Woosnam was just a very natural player. He was explosive and very powerful. He had such a natural swing of the club. He could hit beautiful golf shots. He won a lot of tournaments. I think with him it really came down to putting. If he was hot with the putter he won. When he struggled with the putter, he could not win but the quality of his ball-striking would still take him to a good finish.

Gary Player was my first hero and role-model. He is about my size so his swing was more relevant to me than that of somebody who is taller. He came from a background where it was difficult to play golf and he had to travel long distances to compete with the best in the world – as I have done. He always followed a rigid fitness campaign. He was very determined and achieved a phenomenal amount. He won nine majors and is one of the few who have won all four of the majors.

He was the first overseas player to make a big impact in the USA. He was at his best in a man-to-man contest, as his five wins in the World Matchplay championship show.

I respected him before I met him and gained even more respect for him after I had the opportunity to play that practice round with him in the 1976 Open Championship. He just took so much trouble to help me on that occasion.

I remember meeting Greg Norman when he joined the European tour in the late 1970s. He is the best driver of the ball I have ever seen. That was the first thing I noticed about him, that he hit the ball extremely straight but also very far. If I were to pick out one thing about him it would be that he was, day after day, the longest and straightest driver I have ever seen. Over the years I have seen many players who could hit the ball a long way and I have seen players who could hit the ball straight but not too many who could do both consistently. Greg could do everything in the game really – his long iron play was excellent as was his short game and putting. When he was in form, he could dominate any field and he often did.

For years he was the world-ranked number one player. He was dominant both in Europe and the USA. He was also an extremely popular player both among his colleagues and the fans.

His record in the majors is curious. He only won two (the Open Championship in 1986 and 1993) but I don't know anyone who was in contention so many times. I think he was second in a major eight times. He had some terrible breaks in play-offs, such as when Larry Mize holed his chip in the Masters in 1987 and Bob Tway holed the bunker shot in the PGA in 1986. Greg was there so many times and came away with very little to show for it. He took it on the chin and went on and it didn't seem to affect him. It impressed me that he was always very soft-spoken and didn't use any excuses.

Sergio García has already achieved a great deal for his age. He is one of the best putters that I have seen. He is long for his size. It is impossible to predict the future but I think there is no limit to what he can achieve if he works at it. It would not surprise me if he went a long way in the game.

* * *

Jack Nicklaus was the best player in the world over a significant period. His record of eighteen major victories is unmatched and the span of twenty-four years between first and last is truly remarkable. I admire Jack for what he has achieved. To win the number of majors he has done, he must be not only a great player but also mentally very tough. It is amazing how dominant he was over so many years.

Jack used to drive the ball a very long way. His long iron play was superb. He could hit a one iron longer and softer than almost anyone. He was a very smart player who never beat himself. He was very well organised, who had his game plan – how to play every hole. He was very methodical and deliberate.

He was a tremendously good putter under pressure. He would almost will the ball into the hole. I once talked to him about putting and he told me, 'I am not going to draw the putter back until I know I can make it.' That is an unbelievable statement. That is part of why he was such a great player.

Chapter 19

The 2001 season and beyond

When 2001 started, I had not won a tournament in three years and I was ranked sixty-third in the world. Some golf writers were already working on my obituary: Langer has had a good career; he has been a great player but age has caught up with him. I did not see it quite like that!

Although I had not won for three years, I felt I was playing well during that period and was not far off winning, finishing in second place several times. Often it was just one missed putt, a missed drive, a bad swing, taking the wrong club or a similar misjudgment, which made the difference between winning and finishing down the field.

When I looked back at the end of each day there always seemed to be one or two shots where I was saying to myself, 'How could you have done that?' I just never quite got it all together, although there were several times when I almost did, during those years.

Winning a golf tournament is not an exact science. The funny thing is that sometimes you can win without playing your best, and other times you can play really well but someone just takes one shot less. You can be in the lead and get a bad bounce or someone else holes a pitch and the outcome of the tournament changes.

So my own assessment of that period without a win is that I was very close and just needed some fine tuning. In 2001 I got new golf clubs – all fourteen clubs were new. I changed to a new ball and, as I usually do, I made a few changes to my swing. The changes worked well. Everything just fell into place. What had been missing in the previous three years was there again.

One journalist asked me what was different in 2001. I said, 'I have the same coach, the same caddie, the same wife and still believe in the same God. So I suppose it must be the clubs!'

I played consistently all year. As well as two wins, I had a lot of top-ten finishes, which had been my trademark during the earlier years. I was often in contention and had a lot of good finishes. I felt, in many ways, that 2001 was very similar to my earlier good years.

I had six top-ten finishes in the USA and four more in Europe. I had a solid week in the Masters, finishing nine under par and in sixth place. Unfortunately Tiger was sixteen under.

I have not won in the USA since the 1993 Masters. In 2001 I was second in the Fedex St Jude Classic to Bob Estes and was third three times as well, but a win proved elusive again. Bob opened with a 61 and played extremely well throughout the week. It is tough to win a tournament, leading all the way through. With scores of 69, 65, 68 and 66, I got to within one shot of him. I started the final round five behind but when he bogeyed the fifteenth and I made birdie on the sixteenth, the gap was down to one. On the seventeenth my long birdie putt was on line but stopped a foot short of the hole.

I was third at the Worldcom Classic at Harbour Town where I had won in 1985. I shot three 69s and a 67 but finished one behind José Coceres, who won the play-off, and Billy Mayfair. I was also third in the Players' Championship at Sawgrass. An opening round of 73 left me too much to do and even with rounds of 68, 68 and 67 I was two behind Tiger – who else! That was my third good finish at Sawgrass. I was second to Nick Price in 1993 and to Lee Janzen in 1995.

Sawgrass has a great finish with water on the last three holes. The seventeenth is the hole that everyone knows, the par-three to the island green. The distance on the card is 137 yards but the distance can be fifteen yards different according to whether the pin is front or back. The wind again can make a difference of one or two clubs. I have played as much as a seven and as little as a pitching wedge. If the pin is front half and there isn't much wind it is probably a pitching wedge.

The hole itself is not that hard when there is no wind. The problem is that there is almost always wind, often swirling or coming across so it is more difficult to judge than if it is either with you or against you. There are also so many tall pine trees that you may be sheltered from the wind and not realise how strong it is. The wind is the main reason that so many balls go in the water during the tournament. It is certainly a hole that scares the amateurs. Apparently they fish 150,000 balls out of the water every year!

It is certainly an exciting hole. As you walk onto the tee, the heart is beating a little faster. There are always huge crowds watching. Whenever you see your ball land on the green you feel relieved. But getting it on the green is not enough. You have to be near the pin. The green has three plateaus and you don't want to be on the wrong one.

The seventeenth is a spectacular hole but I think the eighteenth is more scary with water all up the left. On the eighteenth you can bale out and take the water out of play but then you will have such a difficult second shot that you are likely to make bogey or even double. On a calm day the hole is OK and only a bad shot will go wet. When the wind is up, the shot to the green has to be hit with precision to avoid going in the water. You cannot afford to be over-aggressive.

Back in Europe, winning the Dutch Open in Noordwijkse was not only my first win since 1997 but also secured my Ryder Cup place. I was behind all the way. In the final round the fourteenth was the turning point. I played the fourteenth very badly but managed to hole from twelve feet for bogey. That left me two behind with four to play. I birdied the fifteenth, sixteenth and seventeenth to tie with Warren Bennett. I parred the first extra hole, leaving Warren a birdie putt to win. Sadly for him he three-putted.

I also won my own tournament, the Linde German Masters. I was twenty-two under par and beat John Daly and Fredrik Jacobson by one. That was my eleventh European tour victory in Germany. I kept the excitement going to the end by stopping my approach to the seventy-first hole one foot short of water!

I came third in the Open Championship. I was also third at the Nedbank Golf Challenge (Sun City), three shots behind the winner Sergio García. This was my fourteenth appearance at Sun City. Apparently I hold the record for most – 38 – sub-par rounds in the tournament. Both the records I previously held for the lowest and highest scores have thankfully now been broken.

In 2001 I was elected to the World Golf Hall of Fame. This was a tremendous honour, especially to be the first German to receive it. Throughout my career I have striven to achieve a level of consistency, and for this to be recognised in this way means a great deal to me. To join the many outstanding players and great people who are already in the Hall of Fame, people for whom I have so much respect, is truly a privilege.

I finished 2001 ranked thirteenth in the world. People sometimes ask me if the players take the rankings seriously. I think the answer is yes, although it took a while for the world rankings to gain the players' confidence. Sometimes it seemed that US events were too heavily weighted; then it seemed to favour Europeans. But now they seem to have found a formula that is fair for all parts of the world. To prove my point, the rankings are now recognised and used by the controlling bodies and major tournament organisers. As I look at the rankings now, I can't really think of anyone who seems significantly in the wrong place.

One good aspect of the current rankings is that in deciding how many points a particular tournament should carry, they look at the strength of the field. Everybody knows that the majors are the hardest to win and have most of the world's top hundred players playing. So clearly the majors must carry more points.

You can have two regular tournaments in the same week, one with fifty of the world's top players and another with only ten. Again, it is right that the player who wins the first tournament, beating fifty of the world's top players, gets more points than the person winning the lesser tournament. This is now happening.

At the end of the year I spent a few days with my coach to decide what needed to be changed, to be improved. After that I needed a lot of time on the practice ground to try to work these changes into my game. The older you get and the longer you have played the game in a certain way, the more difficult it is to work changes in your grip, your swing, etc. Habits are so ingrained that it takes a long time to work it all through.

Some people find it difficult to understand why I should want to make changes. But even though 2001 was a very successful year, I still felt that I needed to make changes. I still felt that I could do better. There were aspects of my play that I was not happy with.

In 2002 I was thirty-second in the Masters. I liked the changes they made to the course. I think it made it fairer for everyone. A number of bunkers, which the long hitters could previously carry, are now in play for everyone. There are three holes I was less happy with – nine, fourteen and eighteen. I feel those greens are a bit small and not designed for an approach with a long iron. If the holes were 20 yards shorter it would be fine.

The hole that did me most damage that week was the fifteenth. It is the par five with water protecting the green. In the first round I came to the fifteenth three under. I went for the green with my second shot, hitting a three iron. I hit it well and it landed on the green but rolled back into the water. Another yard and I would have been putting for eagle. As it was I took seven. Next day I did exactly the same thing, this time with a five iron.

If you put me in that position again, I would hit the same club in the same way each time – it might go in the water again but it might stay on the green, giving me an eagle putt. Even two birdies would have saved me 5 or 6 shots. It was quite a harsh penalty for missing the target by no more than a metre. But that's golf!

The following week I was fourth in the Worldcom Classic at Harbour Town, three shots behind Justin Leonard. On the first round I was three under with three to play but finished with three bogeys – 5, 4, 5. Next day I finished 3, 3, 3 for a 65! I played well but never quite closed the gap on Justin.

The season ended with a win in the Volvo Masters. I started with two 71s and at the halfway stage was seven behind Angel Cabrera who had opened with a 63. A 72 in the third round left me four behind. That was a disappointing score as I was one under with three to play but dropped shots at 16 and 17.

Nothing much happened on nine but I managed to eagle ten, and birdies at thirteen and seventeen left me four under par. I thought I might need a birdie on eighteen to make the play-off. My putt just missed but a par was enough to leave me three under par and level with Colin Montgomerie.

Before the play-off could start Colin had to speak to the referee about an incident on the tenth hole where TV footage suggested that his ball might have moved after he addressed it. The film was inconclusive and the play-off began.

The first extra hole – the eighteenth – was halved in par fours. I was on in two and two putted. Colin missed the green but chipped close and holed the putt. The second extra hole was the tenth. We were both on in two but neither of us could make the birdie.

We went to the eighteenth tee but it was already pretty dark. There was no way we could continue. There were two options – come back in the morning, which would have provided an anticlimax to a great championship, or share the victory. I think we both agreed that the latter was the appropriate thing to do.

It was also a great end to the European season to share the win with Colin as we had played together so much in the Ryder Cup. And it got me into the record books as the only player on the European tour to share two tournaments, having done the same in the 1986 Trophée Lancôme when Seve and I had to stop because of darkness.

I couldn't get away from Colin. Four weeks later I was fourth equal in the Target World Challenge at Sherwood Country Club in California with rounds of 72, 65, 67, 69. Fourth equal with a certain Colin Montgomerie!

I am always trying to improve. I remember one week I played at Bay Hill, where I got in thirteen greenside bunkers and got up and down every time. The following week I turned up with two new sand-wedges. Peter looked at me in disbelief – wasn't 100 per cent good enough for me? I explained that I was looking for a club that would be better from 90 yards. Again, after I won the Masters, I tried a new putter in the pro-am the next week, in case it was better.

Willi, my coach, always tells me that he wants me still to be playing good golf in fifteen years' time. One of the things I need to do to achieve that is to make changes that relieve the pressure on my back. So it is a combination of two factors – I want to play better, to achieve better results, to stay competitive and at the same time I need to have a technique that puts the minimum pressure on my back and my body. The search for perfection goes on!

Chapter 20

The Ryder Cup 2002

The 2002 Ryder Cup was an unusual event. It was really the 2001 Ryder Cup which had, of course, been postponed because of the events of September 11. In fact, all the official merchandise said 2001! Over the year there had been a lot of press speculation about whether the teams should have been changed. Some newspapers delighted in highlighting how far certain players had fallen in the world rankings in the twelve-month period. I said all along that the twenty-four players had earned their places and it would have been unfair to take anyone out.

2002 had not been my best-ever year – I hadn't won a tournament. I had played solid golf, making the cut in all four majors. My form coming into the Ryder Cup had been good. I finished second in the BMW International Open in Munich – the only tournament in Germany that I have never won – with a score of 20 under, but Thomas Björn played better and was 24 under. I was tenth in the Linde German Masters at 15 under. (That week I spoke at a dinner in Cologne to launch the German edition of this book.) I was 8 under at the WGC American Express Championship in Ireland, which Tiger won, in my last tournament before the Ryder Cup.

We arrived at the Belfry on the Monday and had three full

days before the match started on the Friday. During the period everyone in the press was trying to guess who would play with whom. From conversations I had had with our captain Sam Torrance, I had a feeling I was going to play with Colin Montgomerie. That was confirmed when we were asked to play together in the practice rounds. We had played together in 1991 and 1997 in the Ryder Cup and we always got along well, winning three out of four matches together.

The way it works is that Sam sets the groups for practice, telling us 'I want you and you to play against him and him'. We were told one day to play four-balls and another time to play foursomes. On Thursday we were to play nine holes in the morning, and then in the afternoon it was up to us to decide whether we wanted to play nine more holes, hit balls or just take it easy. Every player has his own routine for preparing for a tournament.

I had also told Sam that I didn't think I could play all four matches in the pairs without being too exhausted for the singles. So we agreed I should play three. Sam decided to play everyone before the singles, which I think is the right approach. It was good that Sam told everyone at the beginning of the week that they would play at least once in the foursomes or four-balls, otherwise players can get anxious about whether or not they will play. He asked us all for our preferences in partners, which again was a great thing to do. Of course we all knew that at the end of the day it was his decision.

I woke up on Thursday morning with a problem. I couldn't turn my head very well to the left – I had a very tight muscle on my left side. And I was actually in question even to play on Friday morning, but I got some help from the physios and was able to play. It improved to where I was 90 per cent fit.

And so, after all the waiting, Friday morning came, and Tiger and Paul Azinger got the proceedings started – in Ryder Cup the visitors always have the honour on the first tee – in their match with Darren and Thomas. Colin and I were out third against Scott Hoch and Jim Furyk.

I holed a twenty-footer on the second to put us ahead. Colin birdied the par five third to put us two up. Furyk birdied the fifth to cut our lead but I managed a birdie on six to win the hole. Colin birdied seven and eight for a half and a win. With Hoch winning the ninth with a birdie we reached the turn two up. The tenth and eleventh were halved, then Colin put us three up on the 208-yard twelfth with a tee shot to twelve feet. I birdied fourteen for a win to leave us four up and four to play. A half at the fifteenth secured our win.

I was happy with how I had played. I was about three under and Colin about four under – it is always an estimate in match-play when not every ball is holed. The important thing was that Colin and I played well as a team, with one of us making a birdie at nine of the fifteen holes. It was a good morning for Europe with a 3–1 lead after the four-balls.

In the afternoon foursomes Colin and I were again out third against Phil Mickelson and David Toms. When you play foursomes, of course, you play alternate shots with one ball. That can be a problem as each player is used to a particular ball in tournaments. For example, I use a Ben Hogan ball and Colin uses a Callaway. One of us has to agree to play an unfamiliar ball. Colin practised with the Ben Hogan ball all week and was happy to use it in our two foursomes matches. Of course that suited me but he seemed to play pretty well with it too.

I hit a good approach on the second and Colin holed to put us ahead, but they squared it at the third. On the fifth I holed for birdie to put us ahead again. At the sixth the Americans found the water and we were two up. We went three up at the eight when Monty holed an eighteen-footer for the birdie. The next six holes were halved to leave us in the great position of three up with four to play. Then it all went wrong. The

Americans birdied fifteen, sixteen and seventeen to get back to all square.

It is easy to say that if you are three up you should win but they played very well. We hit three bad tee shots – I hit two bad ones and Monty one bad one – so we could do no better than par on any of these holes. The seventeeth was a difficult hole. The course was set up to make it a difficult drive. The fairway was only about twelve yards wide in the ideal landing area – normally that fairway is twice as wide. The landing area was in the bend of the dog leg and a ball landing on the fairway tended to bounce through and into the rough. The ideal place to land was in the rough over the bunker, with you then hoping it would bounce out of the rough on to the fairway – which didn't happen every time. It is a very tough tee shot. I drove on the seventeenth and found the bunker so we couldn't reach the green in two, which meant that our par was no match for their birdie.

So we came to the eighteenth all square. The eighteenth is a great finishing hole with so many Ryder Cup memories – Christy O'Connor's two iron in 1989 or Sam Torrance's winning putt in 1983. It is 473 yards with two shots over water. How difficult the eighteenth plays depends a lot on the strength and direction of the wind.

If it is downwind, it isn't too difficult because you can aim further left where the fairway is wider, but if you are into the wind you have to hit it towards the bunker and that is where the fairway is the narrowest. You have to carry the water yet stop it short of the bunker. It is an intimidating shot. You have to hit a solid shot on the right line. A bad shot and you are in trouble – too far left or too short and you are in the water, too straight and you are in the bunker, and then you are looking at bogey or double bogey. Even if you play a good drive you are still left with a long second shot over water to a three-tiered green.

* * *

The eighteenth was halved in bogey. Monty hit a good tee shot but my second wasn't good enough, finishing just off the green. His chip went too far and I missed the putt. The Americans were on the green in two but forty yards from the pin. Mickelson decided to pitch rather than putt but they couldn't make four either.

We were disappointed not to win from such a strong position but their comeback was a combination of them playing their best golf of the round over those three holes and us not being able to find the birdie we needed to finish it off. The USA had a better afternoon to leave the score at the end of day one at Europe 4½ USA 3½.

One of the players who had received a lot of criticism in the press over his poor form coming into the Ryder Cup was Lee Westwood. I was personally delighted to see him (and Sergio) record two wins. Again there had been a lot of nonsense in the papers about the USA starting with a five-point lead as no one would beat Tiger. Actually Tiger lost both games on the Friday.

On the Saturday the order was reversed with the foursomes taking place in the morning. Sam kept Monty and me together and again put us on the list third to face the Scotts – Hoch and Verplank. It was a tight match which went all the way to the eighteenth.

We took the lead on the fourth with a solid par and halved the next five holes. We went further ahead at the tenth. The tenth is another of the famous holes at the Belfry, with the green protected by water. This week it was played at 311 yards. It is a hole where the galleries love to see a player try to drive the green. I think Sergio went for the green in his single and both the four-ball matches but there weren't many players who did. In the singles Sergio went for the green, carried the water but finished in an awkward position, could only make 4 and lost the hole to David Toms, who laid up and made 3.

Colin and I decided not to go for the green. We felt that we are both such good wedge players that we could expect to put our second shot within ten to twelve feet of the hole, and if both of us have a putt from that range, then one of us is going to make it. As we made 3 each time we played it, I think it was the right decision. In the foursomes it doesn't make any sense to go for the green from the tee.

I have been asked how many shots I would get on to the green if I had ten shots at it. It is really hard to say. First of all you have to hit the shot well. But even if you do, there is still a big element of luck. You can just clip a branch of a tree on the right, which would knock the ball off course. And even if you land on the green, there is no guarantee that it will stay on there because of the way the green slopes. In the Saturday four-ball David Duval drove the green and Jesper felt he had to go for it too. Jesper hit a great shot, landed on the green but slightly at the wrong angle and his ball rolled into the water.

For me it is never the percentage shot to go for the green from the tee. If you are confident with your wedge as I am, why take on such a risky shot?

To go back to our Saturday foursome, Colin laid up, I hit a wedge to ten feet and Colin holed the putt and we were two up. Unfortunately we lost the eleventh when Scott Verplank holed a monster for birdie. After four halved holes we lost the fifteenth when they made birdie, which we couldn't match. As we walked off the green, I said to Colin, 'We've lost two holes, but we're still level. We're not behind, we're level and we've got three holes to go. Let's go get them. Let's play and win this thing'. He agreed and we decided to look ahead and not to worry about what was past. We focused on the shots we would face until it was over.

On the 564-yard par five seventeenth my tee shot landed on

the fairway and rolled through into the rough. The Americans were in a similar position. We both laid up. Verplank played first and found the fringe. I had a shot of 167 yards and managed to hit it to six feet. Colin's putt won us the hole.

On eighteen Montgomerie and Hoch hit excellent tee shots. My approach found the green but was on the lower tier. Colin hit a great putt which was enough to half the hole and win the match.

So after three matches Colin and I finished with two wins and a half. What is more, we were actually never down in all three matches. Afterwards Colin said to the press, 'I'd like to say I've had Bernhard Langer as my partner, and the whole team would love to play with him. I was lucky enough to have him. I think the whole American team would love to have him as a partner as well. He's so fantastic in pairings and the way Pete Coleman and he work together is great. What is more, he slows me down. I've got great admiration and respect for him. You need both of these in a partner. And I have that in Bernhard. We've played seven times, and lost one in seven. We have a super record. And I hope it's not his last Ryder Cup and we can have another go at it the next time.'

I really appreciated his comments and I felt exactly the same about playing with him. I was thrilled to be with him. I had told my captain, 'I'll play with anybody.' But I was really pleased to be paired with Colin. And as I said, we get along very well. We just seem to gel well together. In the four-ball matches we did extremely well. Whenever he wasn't quite there, I came in. And when I was gone, he was there. It worked out wonderfully.

I am used to having Vikki with me at the Ryder Cup but this year it was a bonus to also have our daughter Jackie and our son Stefan, now they are old enough to know what is going on. First of all they were thrilled to get a few days off school.

Stefan loves watching golf and walking round with me, and Jackie had a good time with the girls. They enjoyed all the functions during the week. Even on the afternoon I didn't play they were out on the course cheering the team on. Stefan came with me to the press centre on Saturday and finished up answering a few questions himself.

The Saturday morning foursomes were shared but USA gained a point lead from the afternoon four-balls to tie the overall score at 8–8 as we entered the final day. For the singles Sam decided to put his strongest players at the top of the order to try to get points on the board early. In contrast Curtis Strange put his three best players – Love, Mickelson and Woods – out last.

I was drawn with Hal Sutton, whom I had beaten in the singles in 1985. We halved the first four holes. At the second I hit a wedge from 120 yards to three feet. However, the putt horseshoed out. I won the fifth after hitting a six-iron approach to four feet. A birdie at six put me two up. Another good approach shot on the eighth put me three up. With me winning the tenth and him the eleventh followed by a half on twelve, I reached the thirteenth still three up. Hal drove out of bounds at thirteen and later conceded the hole. Halves at fourteen and fifteen gave me the match 4 and 3.

I think I played some of my best golf in the singles. I was really happy with my ball striking. I felt I played very well. The official score had me five under but that included two holes conceded before I putted. On the second I had a terrible lip-out. On the eleventh I had a chip that lipped out so it might have been six or seven under. Everyone seemed pleased with me except for Peter Coleman who remarked, 'I wish he played like that when we play for money!'

Colin completed a magnificent week with a 5 and 4 win in the opening singles. We were getting the points but it was going to be close. In the end Paul McGinley was left with a nine-footer. He put a clutch putt in the cup and the Ryder Cup returned to Europe. The final score was 15½ to 12½.

Then we had the closing ceremony and the presentation of the cup. Afterwards we had some more pictures for the press on the putting green. We sprayed some champagne from the roof. Then the whole team went to the press centre for more interviews. That took about an hour.

About 8.30 we went back to the team room, had dinner and watched some of the highlights on TV. Jesper had arranged for some great entertainment but basically we just sat together and celebrated, listened to music, danced a little and enjoyed ourselves. Some of the Americans dropped in and, of course, they were very welcome.

The atmosphere all week was great. I am not aware of any incidents that bothered anyone. The spectators were certainly on our side but they were very fair. The players played in a very sporting way. The captains were great. Everything was very positive and the game of golf was the real winner. And that is the way it should be. The Ryder Cup remains the most important team event in golf but, after all, it is only a game of golf. It isn't a matter of life and death. I think that is what Samuel Ryder had in mind.

The galleries were awesome. They've been awesome most years. But this year they were just tremendous. Everywhere as soon as you walked off the tee or hit a decent shot they would cheer. They were cheering when you walked along. They must have had sore hands because they were just clapping the whole time, from tee box down to the green. And you could definitely tell by the noise level whether Europe had won a hole or whether the Americans had won a hole. It was just fantastic. I think they were very fair. There were very, very few occasions when I heard that somebody was actually excited that the

Americans might have hit a bad shot or hit it in the water or something like that. You heard very little of that.

The players, too, were excellent. It was really pretty fair and gentlemanly. And that's the way it should be. We don't like to lose. Nobody likes to lose, and it means a lot to everyone out there. But the players were very fair to each other, and that was good to see.

I must also pay tribute to Sam Torrance, who did an excellent job. Sam really wanted to win the match. It was obvious that it meant a lot to him but he was fun to be around. He included everyone. He made a point of talking to all the players, sharing his plans with us and asking our opinions. As I said earlier, I thought he was right to get everyone playing before the singles.

It was such an incredible week. It was my tenth Ryder Cup and this certainly ranks among the best, even though I've been on the winning team five and a half times now. It's been awesome. I don't think there are many Ryder Cups left in me but perhaps I can still play a part in 2004.

Chapter 21

The future

If my body holds up I would expect to play the seniors' tour. If I still have the desire to compete and still enjoy playing the game of golf – and I expect to – then you will see me on the seniors' tour. I don't think there is much chance of me losing the desire to compete. Once you have won, that's what you live for. You want to win again. There is nothing like winning. They say nobody remembers second or third and that's the truth.

I don't travel all over the world just to be part of the tournament. I would not play if I did not have the drive to want to win. I am the kind of person who always gives 100 per cent. With me it is at times too intense and sometimes I have to slow down and tell myself it is only a golf tournament, not life and death.

It is more a question of how healthy will I be. From the age of fifty to fifty-five there is a lot of money to be made on the seniors' tour. You are one of the youngest, strongest and longest players at that stage. Beyond fifty-five it seems to be more difficult to be very successful.

I am going to be playing against the guys in my age group, the same guys I have competed against all my life – Nick Faldo, Greg Norman, Nick Price, Seve and so on. I have enjoyed competing with them on the regular tour and I guess it won't be much different on the seniors'.

Before that I still have ambitions to win another major. It

176

doesn't get easier with age. When you think that Nicklaus was the oldest player ever to win a major at forty-six, then I have to conclude that there may not be many years left. There is still life left. It all depends on how keen you still remain after so many years as a pro. It also depends on how focused you remain.

I don't see the need to retire. I like working, so why retire? Obviously, I could spend more time with my family, which would be nice, but every day of the year? I'm not sure my life would be fulfilled. There is still a part of me that is used to working and needs the adrenaline and the excitement that comes with it.

I wouldn't enjoy sitting on the beach all day, as most people would. That would be about the worst punishment you could give me. I'm too active. I need to be doing something.

I have a family. I have four kids. I have an office in my home, where I spend hours dealing with a mountain of paperwork. I did none of that fifteen years ago. I have two managers as well as my brother working for me. There is so much that I need to do. But I am still first and foremost a golfer.

I am still determined. I know I can improve my game. I can improve my technique. What I really want is to hit more fairways and greens because that is much more relaxing than scrambling around.

I have a lot of experience. I have been a pro for almost thirty years. I may not hit it as far as the young kids on the tour but I know shots that they don't. I have repeated my swing millions of times. They have not done that. They are not old enough. So there are advantages and disadvantages in youth and experience. I think if I look after myself and commit the time to practice and fitness, then I can stay competitive for a number of years yet.

I would like to win the Open Championship. I go out there to practise or play, every day trying the best I can. Sometimes in a match the best is 65 and sometimes it's a 78. Personally I'd like to be a good husband and father, and hope my family and

I can keep healthy for many years and that there are no tragedies. And I hope we can keep our family unit together. There are so many divorces these days and kids are suffering from it.

Jesus said, 'Don't worry about tomorrow. It will take care of itself. You have enough to worry about today.' That is good advice. It is only with the strength of God that I have been able to endure the problems I have faced and still remain so content. I believe it is not what you achieve but what you overcome that is the telling factor. My confidence in the future is based on the knowledge that God will continue to be with me.

I hope this has given you a flavour of my life. You see, I was twenty-eight years old and had basically achieved almost everything that I wanted to and dreamed of. It was then that I realised that material things don't make you happy and that there must be more in this life than just accumulating money in the bank or cars or houses or whatever. You just want more, more, more and are never satisfied.

As I explained, through a Bible study on the US tour, I came to know Jesus Christ as my personal saviour and that made all the difference. Sometimes we get overwhelmed by the things the world expects from us or the things we want to achieve ourselves. As a Christian, God is my number one priority and whenever I fail in this world or have hard times, I just remind myself of what Jesus did for me on the cross and how fortunate and blessed I am to know him personally and that he has taken all my sins away. No matter what might happen in this world, it's not going to dampen my joy of going to see him personally in heaven.

A journalist once asked me, 'What would you have as your epitaph?'

I replied, 'It doesn't make any difference what's written on your gravestone. It's only important that your soul's going to heaven.'

Appendix

Bernhard Langer Career Record

Biographical/Personal details

Date of birth	27 August 1957
Turned professional	1972
Married	to Vikki (1984)
Children	Jackie (1986), Stefan (1990), Christina (1993), Jason (2000)

Tournament Wins

1975
German National Open

1977
German National Open

1979
Cacharel World Under-25 Championship
German National Open

1980
Dunlop Masters
Colombian Open

1981
Bob Hope British Classic
German Open

1982
Lufthansa German Open

1983
Italian Open
Glasgow Golf Classic
St Mellion Timeshare TPC
Casio World Open
Johnnie Walker Tournament

1984
Peugeot Open de France
KLM Dutch Open
Carroll's Irish Open
Benson and Hedges Spanish Open
German National Open

1985
US Masters
Lufthansa German Open
Panasonic European Open
Sea Pines Heritage Classic
Australian Masters
Sun City Million Dollar Challenge
German National Open

1986
German Open
Trophée Lancôme
German National Open

1987
Whyte & Mackay PGA Championship
Carroll's Irish Open
German National Open

1988
Epson Grand Prix of Europe
German National Open

1989
Peugeot Spanish Open
German Masters
German National Open

1990
Cepsa Madrid Open
Austrian Open
German National Open

1991
Benson and Hedges International Open
Mercedes German Masters
Sun City Million Dollar Challenge
Hong Kong Open
German National Open

1992
Heineken Dutch Open
Honda Open
German National Open

1993
US Masters
Volvo PGA Championship
Volvo German Open

1994
Murphy's Irish Open
Volvo Masters

1995
Volvo PGA Championship
Deutsche Bank Open TPC of Europe
Smurfit European Open

1996
Alfred Dunhill Masters, Hong Kong

1997
Conte of Florence Italian Open
Benson and Hedges International Open
Chemapol Trophy Czech Open
Linde German Masters
Argentinian Masters

2001
TNT Dutch Open
Linde German Masters

2002
Volvo Masters

Tournaments in Germany

	German Open	German Masters	BMW International	Deutsche Bank Open	Honda Open
1974	MC*	–	–	–	–
1975	MC	–	–	–	–
1976	32	–	–	–	–
1977	MC	–	–	–	–
1978	MC	–	–	–	–
1979	30	–	–	–	–
1980	43	–	–	–	–
1981	1	–	–	–	–
1982	1	–	–	–	–
1983	16	–	–	–	–
1984	18	–	–	–	–
1985	1	–	–	–	–
1986	1	–	–	–	–
1987	9	2	–	–	–
1988	29	31	–	–	–
1989	5	1	MC	–	–
1990	19	2	–	–	–
1991	22	1	15	–	–
1992	34	2	2	–	1
1993	1	4	3	–	5
1994	2	34	14	–	5
1995	37	2	2	1	–
1996	37	23	16	15	–
1997	4	1	12	MC	–
1998	13	15	4	4	–
1999	32	9	15	11	–
2000	–	6	2	MC	–
2001	–	1	16	47	–
2002	–	10	2	60	–

Overall record in Germany – 11 victories, 9 second place finishes and 32 top ten finishes – in addition to 12 German National Open wins.

*MC = Missed Cut

The Majors

	US Masters	US Open	The Open	USPGA
1976	–	–	MC*	–
1977	–	–	–	–
1978	–	–	MC	–
1979	–	–	–	–
1980	–	–	51	–
1981	–	–	2	–
1982	MC	MC	13	–
1983	–	–	56	–
1984	31	–	2	–
1985	1	MC	3	32
1986	16	8	3	MC
1987	7	4	17	21
1988	9	MC	68	MC
1989	26	59	78	61
1990	7	MC	48	MC
1991	32	MC	9	MC
1992	31	23	59	40
1993	1	MC	3	MC
1994	25	23	60	25
1995	31	36	24	–
1996	36	MC	MC	76
1997	7	MC	38	23
1998	39	MC	MC	–
1999	11	–	18	61
2000	28	MC	11	46
2001	6	40	3	77
2002	32	35	28	23

His run of making 19 successive cuts in the US Masters is the longest current sequence in the tournament. He is 4 behind Gary Player's all-time record of 23 successive Masters cuts.

*MC = Missed Cut

World Ranking

The official World Ranking was introduced in 1986 and Bernhard was the first player to reach the top. His position in the ranking at 30 June each year is as follows:

1986	1
1987	3
1988	4
1989	20
1990	13
1991	8
1992	5
1993	2
1994	4
1995	4
1996	9
1997	17
1998	23
1999	36
2000	64
2001	47
2002	23

European Order of Merit Summary

Year	Order of Merit Winnings	Ranking Position
2002	€ 947,232	19
2001	€1,577,130	6
2000	€ 759,903	19
1999	€ 496,608	15
1998	£ 262,347	18
1997	£ 692,398	2
1996	£ 152,348	39
1995	£ 655,854	3
1994	£ 635,483	2
1993	£ 469,570	4
1992	£ 488,913	2
1991	£ 372,703	3
1990	£ 320,450	4
1989	£ 205,195	7
1988	£ 66,368	30
1987	£ 141,394	5
1986	£ 124,068	–
1985	£ 115,716	2
1984	£ 139,344	1
1983	£ 73,734	3
1982	£ 43,848	6
1981	£ 81,036	1
1980	£ 32,395	9
1979	£ 7,972	56
1978	£ 7,006	40
1977	£ 691	204
1976	£ 2,130	90

Ryder Cup record

1981 at Walton Heath
Match Result: USA 18½ Europe 9½

Foursomes Day 1: Bernhard Langer and Manúel Piñero lost to Larry Nelson and Lee Trevino by 1 hole

Four-balls Day 2: Bernhard Langer and Manúel Piñero beat Ray Floyd and Hale Irwin, 2 and 1

Foursomes Day 2: Bernhard Langer and Manúel Piñero lost to Jack Nicklaus and Tom Watson, 3 and 2

Singles: Bernhard Langer halved with Bruce Lietzke

1983 at PGA National, Palm Beach Gardens
Match Result: USA 14½ Europe 13½

Foursomes Day 1: Bernhard Langer and Nick Faldo beat Lanny Wadkins and Craig Stadler, 4 and 2

Four-balls Day 1: Bernhard Langer and Nick Faldo lost to Tom Watson and Jay Haas, 2 and 1

Four-balls Day 2: Bernhard Langer and Nick Faldo beat Ben Crenshaw and Calvin Peete, 4 and 2

Foursomes Day 2: Bernhard Langer and Nick Faldo beat Tom Kite and Ray Floyd, 3 and 2

Singles: Bernhard Langer beat Gill Morgan by 2 holes

1985 at the Belfry
Match Result: Europe 16½ USA 11½

Foursomes Day 1: Bernhard Langer and Nick Faldo lost to Calvin Peete and Tom Kite, 3 and 2

Four-balls Day 1: Bernhard Langer and José María Cañizares halved with Craig Stadler and Hal Sutton

Four-balls Day 2: Bernhard Langer and Sandy Lyle halved with Craig Stadler and Curtis Strange

Foursomes Day 2: Bernhard Langer and Ken Brown beat Ray Floyd and Lanny Wadkins, 3 and 2

Singles: Bernhard Langer beat Hal Sutton 5 and 4

1987 at Muirfield Village
Match Result: Europe 15 USA 13

Foursomes Day 1: Bernhard Langer and Ken Brown lost to Hal Sutton and Dan Pohl, 2 and 1

Four-balls Day 1: Bernhard Langer and Sandy Lyle beat Andy Bean and Mark Calcavecchia by 1 hole

Foursomes Day 2: Bernhard Langer and Sandy Lyle beat Lanny Wadkins and Larry Nelson, 2 and 1

Four-balls Day 2: Bernhard Langer and Sandy Lyle beat Lanny Wadkins and Larry Nelson by 1 hole

Singles: Bernhard Langer halved with Larry Nelson

1989 at the Belfry
Match Result: Europe 14 USA 14

Foursomes Day 1: Bernhard Langer and Ronan Rafferty lost to Ken Green and Mark Calcavecchia, 2 and 1

Four-balls Day 2: Bernhard Langer and José María Cañizares lost to Tom Kite and Mark McCumber, 2 and 1

Singles: Bernhard Langer lost to Chip Beck, 3 and 1

1991 at Kiawah Island
Match Result: USA 14½ Europe 13½

Foursomes Day 1: Bernhard Langer and Mark James lost to Ray Floyd and Fred Couples, 2 and 1

Four-balls Day 2: Bernhard Langer and Colin Montgomerie beat Steve Pate and Corey Pavin, 2 and 1

Singles: Bernhard Langer halved with Hale Irwin

1993 at the Belfry
Match Result: USA 15 Europe 13

Foursomes Day 1: Bernhard Langer and Ian Woosnam beat Paul Azinger and Payne Stewart, 7 and 5

Four-balls Day 1: Bernhard Langer and Barry Lane lost to Lanny Wadkins and Corey Pavin, 4 and 2

Foursomes Day 2: Bernhard Langer and Ian Woosnam beat Paul Azinger and Fred Couples, 2 and 1

Singles: Bernhard Langer lost to Tom Kite, 5 and 3

1995 at Oak Hill Country Club, Rochester NY
Match Result: Europe 14½ USA 13½

Foursomes Day 1: Bernhard Langer and Per-Ulrik Johansson beat Ben Crenshaw and Curtis Strange, by 1 hole

Four-balls Day 1: Bernhard Langer and Per-Ulrik Johansson lost to Corey Pavin and Phil Mickelson, 6 and 4

Foursomes Day 2: Bernhard Langer and David Gilford beat Corey Pavin and Tom Lehman, 4 and 3

Four-balls Day 2: Bernhard Langer and Nick Faldo lost to Corey Pavin and Loren Roberts by 1 hole

Singles: Bernhard Langer lost to Corey Pavin, 3 and 2

1997 at Valderrama
Match Result: Europe 14½ USA 13½

Foursomes Day 1: Bernhard Langer and Colin Montgomerie lost to Tiger Woods and Mark O'Meara, 3 and 2

Four-balls Day 1: Bernhard Langer and Colin Montgomerie beat Tiger Woods and Mark O'Meara, 5 and 3

Foursomes Day 2: Bernhard Langer and Colin Montgomerie beat Lee Janzen and Jim Furyk by 1 hole

Singles: Bernhard Langer beat Brad Faxon, 2 and 1

2002 at the Belfry
Match result Europe 15½ USA 12½

Four-balls Day 1: Bernhard Langer and Colin Montgomerie beat Scott Hoch and Jim Furyk, 4 and 3

Foursomes Day 1: Bernhard Langer and Colin Montgomerie halved with Phil Mickelson and David Toms

Foursomes Day 2: Bernhard Langer and Colin Montgomerie beat Scott Hoch and Scott Verplank by 1 hole

Singles: Bernhard Langer beat Hal Sutton, 4 and 3

Overall Ryder Cup record

Played	Won	Halved	Lost	Points	Win %
42	21	6	15	24	57

24 Ryder Cup points gained is the second highest ever European score behind Nick Faldo's 25.

His 11 Foursomes wins is a Ryder Cup record.

Miscellaneous Records

Low rounds
60   Berliner G & CC, Motzener See, Linde German Masters, 1997 [–12]

62   Benson and Hedges Spanish Open, El Saler, Valencia, 1984 [–10]

62   Gleneagles, Bell's Scottish Open, 1992 [–8]

62   Valderrama, Volvo Masters, 1994 [–9]

63   Royal Dublin GC, Carroll's Irish Open, 1985 [–8]

64   Royal Zoute, Knokke, Belgium, Alfred Dunhill Open, 1993 [–7]

64   Gardagolf Brescia, Conte de Florence Italian Open, 1997 [–8]

64   Golf Club Gut Lärchenhof, Cologne, Linde German Masters, 2001 [–8]

Holes in one

Australian Masters at Huntingdale 1985 – 12th hole, final round

Volvo Masters in Montecastillo 1998 – 14th hole, third round

Team competition

Alfred Dunhill Cup (Germany) 1992, 1994, 2000

World Cup (Germany) 1976, 1977, 1978, 1979, 1980, 1990 [Germany winners], 1991, 1992, 1993, 1994, 1996

Hennessey Cognac Cup (Europe) 1976, 1978, 1980, 1982

Seve Ballesteros Trophy (Europe) 2000

4 Tours World Championship (Europe) 1985, 1986, 1987, 1989, 1990

UBS Warburg Cup (Rest of the World) 2001, 2002

Glossary

2 and 1 – a result in *matchplay* two holes up with one to play (the winner is two holes up and the loser has run out of holes in which to catch up!)

address the ball – get into position to hit the ball

air-shot – an attempted shot that doesn't make contact with the ball. It still counts as a shot

approach – a short shot played from the fairway to the green

birdie – a hole played in one shot under *par*

bogey – a hole played in one stroke over *par*

carry – the distance the ball travels through the air before touching the ground

chip – a lofted approach shot to the green in which the run-on of the ball is relied on

club – the instrument used to strike the ball. A player is allowed a maximum of 14 clubs, which fall into three categories: woods (traditionally made of wood but now more often of metal), irons and a putter

cut – in a professional golf *strokeplay* tournament, only the top 60 or so players qualify for the final two of the four rounds. The process of deciding which players qualify is called the cut. Players are said to 'make the cut' or 'miss the cut'

dead – to knock a ball dead (or 'stiff') means to put the ball very close to the *pin*

divot – the piece of turf sliced out of a fairway or other ground when making an iron shot

divot-hole – the hole from which a *divot* is taken

draw – a shot that (for a right-hander) goes from right to left in flight

drop a ball – dropping a ball to replay a shot happens when the original ball has been lost. This incurs a *penalty shot*

drop a shot – to score a *bogey*, one over *par*

duff – to ruin a shot, usually by hitting the ground before connecting with the ball

eagle – a hole completed in two strokes under *par*

fade – a shot that (for a right-hander) goes from left to right in flight

fat – hitting a shot fat means to hit the ground slightly behind the ball

flag (or 'pin') – a stick with a flag on the top that marks the location of the hole on the green

four-ball – a match in which two play against two, with each player hitting a separate ball. The format is *matchplay*, with the lowest score of the four balls winning the hole

foursome – a match in which two play against two and each side plays one ball, taking alternate shots

flyer – a shot from *rough* where the grooves on the club-face do not make contact with the ball. These grooves impart backspin. When no backspin is imparted, the ball flies further, hence a 'flyer'

gimme – a conceded putt when the ball lands *dead* alongside the hole. ('Gimme' is a contracted form of 'Give it to me' based on *matchplay* where a player may give a putt to an opponent, not requiring the opponent to put the ball in the hole.)

handicap – a figure allocated to all golfers so that players of varying standards can play each other. The lower the handicap figure, the better the player

hole – the target on each green is a hole in the ground 108mm in diameter. The word is also used to describe an individual section of the golf course from *tee* to green. A golf-course consists of 18 holes

hole in one – a player's tee-shot that goes straight into the hole

hook – a shot that (for right-handers) starts off right of the target and swings violently left during its flight

lipped out – a putt that hits the hole and runs around it without dropping in

matchplay – a golf match where two players (or two pairs) play against each other. The outcome is decided by who wins the most holes. Strokes are not counted cumulatively

par – the number of shots allotted for any given hole (or the entire course). The par for a hole – 3, 4 or 5 – is determined by the length and always includes two shots on the green

penalty shot – a shot that is added to the player's score for an infringement of the rules

pin – see 'flag'

pitch – a lofted shot that flies in the air all the way to the target, rather than bouncing and running on

play-off – when a *strokeplay* tournament ends with two or more players equal, those players play off to find a winner. Play-offs may be over a set number of holes or to a sudden death in which the first person to win a hole is the winner

rough – longer grass off the fairway from which it is more difficult to hit a shot

shank – a shot in which the ball is propelled at speed almost at right angles to the player, with hardly any forward travel. The ball is hit from the hosel (where the shaft fits into the head of the club), which, because it is round, causes the ball to go sideways

short game – shots around the green

slice – a shot that (for a right-hander) starts left of the target and sweeps back to finish right of it

stiff – see 'dead'

stroke and distance – when a player loses a ball or goes out of bounds, the shot is replayed from the point where the previous one was played. The penalty is called stroke and distance as a stroke is added to the score and the player loses the distance the previous shot travelled

strokeplay – most professional golf tournaments are in strokeplay format, i.e. all the strokes taken are counted cumulatively and the player taking the least strokes to complete the course wins

tee (or **teeing ground**) – area of the course from which a player starts a hole and on which the player is allowed to place the ball on a tee to raise it above the ground

ten-shot rule – a rule in a *strokeplay* tournament that means that all players within 10 shots of the leader make the *cut*

thin – when the ball is struck with the bottom of the club it is said to be caught thin

three putts – one putt too many. *Par* is based on an assumption of two putts

wedge – an iron used for playing short or pitch shots, e.g. a pitching wedge, sand wedge, or lob wedge

yardage – the distance from any given point on a hole to the flag

yips – an involuntary and uncontrollable movement of the muscles, resulting in a fast, jerky, uncontrolled putting stroke

Index of names

Abreu, Francisco 12
Allenby, Robert 99
Aoki, Isao 14
Azinger, Paul 13, 31, 66, 69, 96, 125–7, 107

Baker, Peter 97
Ballesteros, Severiano 20–1, 29–31, 35–7, 44, 46, 54, 66–7, 73, 99–100, 103, 117, 123–4, 154–5, 162, 165
Barnes, Brian 21
Beck, Chip 104–5
Bennett, Warren 162
Björn, Thomas 123, 166, 168
Bland, John 31
Brand, Gordon, Jnr 96
Brown, Ken 17, 30, 63
Brügelman, Jan 10, 13

Cabrera, Angel 164
Campbell, Michael 101
Carrigill, Paul 88
Cejka, Alexander 116
Clampett, Bobby 49
Clark, Howard 17, 34, 36
Clarke, Darren 96, 98, 121, 168
Claydon, Russell 121
Coceres, José 160
Coleman, Peter 25, 28–30, 36, 67, 89, 105, 115–16, 122, 148–9, 165, 172
Coles, Neil 94
Coltart, Andrew 71
Connors, Jimmy 115
Couples, Fred 13, 66, 95, 97
Crenshaw, Ben 43, 47

Daly, John 40, 99, 111, 156, 162
Davis, Rodger 88, 91, 94
Day, Glen 96

de Burgh, Chris 66
Duval, David 13, 56, 171

Els, Ernie 116
Estes, Bob 160

Faldo, Nick 17, 19, 34, 56, 62, 95, 98, 104, 155, 176
Faxon, Brad 70, 121
Fehring, Heinz 7–9
Fernandez, Vicente 31
Floyd, Ray 44, 46, 57, 62, 66
Forsbrand, Anders 96
Forsman, Dan 103–4
Furyk, Jim 95, 168

Gallacher, Bernard 17, 21, 62, 73
García, Sergio 72, 157, 162, 170
Garrido, Antonio 20
Giedeon, Torsten 92
Gillingham, Bruce 66, 69, 89–90, 97
Goosen, Retief 121
Graham, David 54
Gray, Tony 34
Green, Hubert 21
Gühring, Hermann 90

Hallberg, Gary 43
Harrington, Padraig 118, 121
Hay, Alex 14
Hayes, Dale 95
Hoch, Scott 168, 170, 172
Hoffman, Willi 8, 33, 47, 165
Hogan, Ben 107–8
Hopkins, John 88
Horton, Tommy 29

Ingles, David 48
Irwin, Hale 19, 62, 66–7

Jacklin, Tony 23, 28, 56, 72
Jacobs, John 72
Jacobson, Fredrik 162
Jacobson, Peter 125
James, Mark 17, 20, 34, 66, 71, 73, 96
Janzen, David 69
Janzen, Lee 69, 102, 160
Jiménez, Miguel Angel 121
Johannsson, Per-Ulrik 101
Johnstone, Tony 87–8
Jones, Bobby 40

Kang, Wook Soon 115
Karlsson, Robert 71
Kessler, Manfred 10
Kite, Tom 69–70
König, Gerhard 10
Kostis, Peter 143

Lane, Barry 101
Langer, Christina 33, 132–4, 138
Langer, Erwin (brother) 2–4, 6, 93, 121,
  128
Langer, Erwin (father) 1–2, 6–7
Langer, Jackie 33, 56, 86, 121, 132–4,
  137–8, 172–3
Langer, Jason 132
Langer, Maria (niece) 121
Langer, Maria (sister) 2–3, 6, 121
Langer, Stefan 33, 132–5, 172–3
Langer, Vikki 32–4, 47–51, 56, 65, 86, 121,
  131–5, 137, 172
Langer, Wally 2, 7, 106
Leaney, Stephen 123
Lendl, Ivan 58, 120
Leonard, Justin 72, 164
Levenson, Gavin 97
Lietzke, Bruce 62
Locke, Bobby 19
Longmuir, Bill 28, 87
Lopez, Nancy 29
Love, Davis 42, 97, 111, 123, 173
Lyle, Sandy 21, 55–6, 62–4, 113, 156

Maggert, Jeff 122
Mahaffey, John 17, 89
Maharaj, Sooky 5
Marsh, Graham 34
Mayfair, Billy 160
McGinley, Paul 174
McLean, Michael 38, 96
McNulty, Mark 38, 88
Mickleson, Phil 40, 168, 170, 173

Miller, Johnny 17
Mize, Larry 103, 157
Montgomerie, Colin 66, 70, 100, 116, 123,
  126, 149, 164–5, 167–73
Moody, Larry 49–51, 69, 129
Morgan, Gill 62
Mosely, Jarrod 121
Mouland, Mark 101
Musgrove, Dave 148–9

Nance, Jim 46
Nelson, Bryron 40
Nelson, Larry 61, 64
Nicklaus, Jack 5–6, 15, 17, 35, 40, 45, 61–2,
  91, 158, 177
Norman, Greg 21, 28, 36, 55–6, 103–4, 122,
  156, 176
North, Andy 17

O'Connor, Christy, Jnr 28, 169
Ogle, Brett 91
Olazábal, José María 72, 89, 116, 120
O'Leary, John 17
O'Meara, Mark 70
Oosterhuis, Peter 24

Palmer, Arnold 6, 28, 40, 154
Paramor, John 100, 123
Parnevik, Jesper 45, 71–2, 171, 174
Pate, Steve 66
Pavin, Corey 36, 56, 66, 69, 87, 102
Piñero, Manúel 17, 61–2
Pinney, Mark 89
Player, Gary 14–15, 156–7
Pollard, Eddie 20
Price, Nick 99, 160, 176

Rivero, José 34
Rogers, Bill 53, 56
Ryder, Samuel 174

Sarazen, Gene 43
Schofield, Ken 125
Seidel, Manfred 3
Simpson, Scott 57
Singh, Vijay 93, 100
Snead, Sam 437
Stadler, Craig 44, 63
Stewart, Payne 69, 89, 121, 125–7
Stewart, Tracey 125
Strange, Curtis 44, 46, 63, 103, 173
Strüver, Sven 97
Sutton, Hal 62, 173

Index of names

Toms, David 168, 171
Torrance, Sam 20, 72–3, 121, 167, 169–70, 173, 175
Trevino, Lee 13, 17, 61
Tway, Bob 157

Valerian, Harry 44
Verplank, Scott 170–2

Wadkins, Bobby 17, 38

Wadkins, Lanny 64, 91
Waites, Brian 17
Watson, Tom 28, 54, 61–2
Westner, Wayne 116
Westwood, Lee 117–19, 170
Williams, Frank 48
Wingfield Digby, Andrew 89
Woods, Tiger 40–1, 70, 111–13, 153–4, 156, 160, 166–7, 170, 173
Woosnam, Ian 69, 117, 123, 156